OPPOSING
VIEWPOINTS®
SERIES

Homosexuality

Other Books of Related Interest:

At Issue Series
Are Adoption Policies Fair?
Gay Marriage

Current Controversies
Gays in the Military

Global Viewpoints
Civil Liberties

Introducing Issues with Opposing Viewpoints
Sexual Orientation

Issues That Concern You
Adoption

Opposing Viewpoints
AIDS
Gay Parenting

Social Issues in Literature
Gender in Lorraine Hansberry's *A Raisin in the Sun*

"Congress shall make no law . . . abridging the freedom of speech, or of the press."

First Amendment to the US Constitution

The basic foundation of our democracy is the First Amendment guarantee of freedom of expression. The Opposing Viewpoints series is dedicated to the concept of this basic freedom and the idea that it is more important to practice it than to enshrine it.

OPPOSING VIEWPOINTS® SERIES

Homosexuality

David Haugen and Susan Musser, Book Editors

GREENHAVEN PRESS
A part of Gale, Cengage Learning

GALE
CENGAGE Learning®

Detroit • New York • San Francisco • New Haven, Conn • Waterville, Maine • London

GALE
CENGAGE Learning·

Elizabeth Des Chenes, *Director, Publishing Solutions*

© 2013 Greenhaven Press, a part of Gale, Cengage Learning.

Gale and Greenhaven Press are registered trademarks used herein under license.

For more information, contact:
Greenhaven Press
27500 Drake Rd.
Farmington Hills, MI 48331-3535
Or you can visit our Internet site at gale.cengage.com

Articles in Greenhaven Press anthologies are often edited for length to meet page requirements. In addition, original titles of these works are changed to clearly present the main thesis and to explicitly indicate the author's opinion. Every effort is made to ensure that Greenhaven Press accurately reflects the original intent of the authors. Every effort has been made to trace the owners of copyrighted material.

Cover image © Nuno Andre/Shutterstock.com.

LIBRARY OF CONGRESS CATALOGING-IN-PUBLICATION DATA

Homosexuality / David Haugen and Susan Musser, book editors.
        pages cm. -- (Opposing viewpoints)
    Includes bibliographical references and index.
    ISBN 978-0-7377-6324-9 (hbk.) -- ISBN 978-0-7377-6325-6 (pbk.)
    1. Homosexuality. I. Haugen, David M., 1969- editor of compilation. II. Musser, Susan, editor of compilation.
    HQ75.15.H66 2013
    306.76'6--dc23
                                                                2012040675

Printed in the United States of America
1 2 3 4 5   17 16 15 14 13

Contents

Why Consider Opposing Viewpoints?

> "The only way in which a human being can make some approach to knowing the whole of a subject is by hearing what can be said about it by persons of every variety of opinion and studying all modes in which it can be looked at by every character of mind. No wise man ever acquired his wisdom in any mode but this."
>
> John Stuart Mill

In our media-intensive culture it is not difficult to find differing opinions. Thousands of newspapers and magazines and dozens of radio and television talk shows resound with differing points of view. The difficulty lies in deciding which opinion to agree with and which "experts" seem the most credible. The more inundated we become with differing opinions and claims, the more essential it is to hone critical reading and thinking skills to evaluate these ideas. Opposing Viewpoints books address this problem directly by presenting stimulating debates that can be used to enhance and teach these skills. The varied opinions contained in each book examine many different aspects of a single issue. While examining these conveniently edited opposing views, readers can develop critical thinking skills such as the ability to compare and contrast authors' credibility, facts, argumentation styles, use of persuasive techniques, and other stylistic tools. In short, the Opposing Viewpoints Series is an ideal way to attain the higher-level thinking and reading skills so essential in a culture of diverse and contradictory opinions.

In addition to providing a tool for critical thinking, Opposing Viewpoints books challenge readers to question their own strongly held opinions and assumptions. Most people form their opinions on the basis of upbringing, peer pressure, and personal, cultural, or professional bias. By reading carefully balanced opposing views, readers must directly confront new ideas as well as the opinions of those with whom they disagree. This is not to argue simplistically that everyone who reads opposing views will—or should—change his or her opinion. Instead, the series enhances readers' understanding of their own views by encouraging confrontation with opposing ideas. Careful examination of others' views can lead to the readers' understanding of the logical inconsistencies in their own opinions, perspective on why they hold an opinion, and the consideration of the possibility that their opinion requires further evaluation.

Evaluating Other Opinions

To ensure that this type of examination occurs, Opposing Viewpoints books present all types of opinions. Prominent spokespeople on different sides of each issue as well as well-known professionals from many disciplines challenge the reader. An additional goal of the series is to provide a forum for other, less known, or even unpopular viewpoints. The opinion of an ordinary person who has had to make the decision to cut off life support from a terminally ill relative, for example, may be just as valuable and provide just as much insight as a medical ethicist's professional opinion. The editors have two additional purposes in including these less known views. One, the editors encourage readers to respect others' opinions—even when not enhanced by professional credibility. It is only by reading or listening to and objectively evaluating others' ideas that one can determine whether they are worthy of consideration. Two, the inclusion of such viewpoints encourages the important critical thinking skill of objectively evaluating an author's credentials and bias. This evaluation will illuminate an author's reasons for taking a particular stance on an issue and will aid in readers' evaluation of the author's ideas.

It is our hope that these books will give readers a deeper understanding of the issues debated and an appreciation of the complexity of even seemingly simple issues when good and honest people disagree. This awareness is particularly important in a democratic society such as ours in which people enter into public debate to determine the common good. Those with whom one disagrees should not be regarded as enemies but rather as people whose views deserve careful examination and may shed light on one's own.

Thomas Jefferson once said that "difference of opinion leads to inquiry, and inquiry to truth." Jefferson, a broadly educated man, argued that "if a nation expects to be ignorant and free . . . it expects what never was and never will be." As individuals and as a nation, it is imperative that we consider the opinions of others and examine them with skill and discernment. The Opposing Viewpoints series is intended to help readers achieve this goal.

David L. Bender and Bruno Leone,
Founders

Introduction

> "Don't misunderstand. I am not here bashing people who are homosexuals, who are lesbians, who are bisexual, who are transgender. We need to have profound compassion for people who are dealing with the very real issue of sexual dysfunction in their life and sexual identity disorders."
>
> —Michele Bachmann,
> EdWatch National Education
> Conference, November 6, 2004

> "Despite the persistence of stereotypes that portray lesbian, gay, and bisexual people as disturbed, several decades of research and clinical experience have led all mainstream medical and mental health organizations in this country to conclude that these orientations represent normal forms of human experience. Lesbian, gay, and bisexual relationships are normal forms of human bonding."
>
> —American Psychological
> Association, "Sexual Orientation
> and Homosexuality," 2008

In his 1886 treatise *Psychopathia Sexualis*, German psychiatrist and professor Richard von Krafft-Ebing compiled a list of sexual aberrations that might help explain the behavior of criminals charged with sex crimes in courts of law. Among the disorders Krafft-Ebing described was homosexuality, a behavior that he believed was governed by misdirected sexual desire—that is, one that eschewed the "normal" goal of procreation. Although Krafft-Ebing initially claimed that homosexuality was a vice that might influence criminal actions, his work was significant in defining homosexuality as a mental pathology and not a religious sin. Up until the mid-to-late nineteenth century, the teachings of the Christian church deeply influenced legal codes, and since the twelfth century, the church had condemned homosexuality as a sin, because it was non-procreative, that in some legal jurisdictions was punishable by death. Krafft-Ebing ignored the issue of "sinfulness" and maintained that homosexuality was a degenerative illness that affected many people. Over time, Krafft-Ebing revised his major work, and in the final edition, he changed his views considerably. After working with many homosexual men that sought his advice and treatment, Krafft-Ebing could find nothing morally degenerate about many of the individuals in his care. By the end of his life, the noted professor advocated that homosexuality be declassified as a criminal behavior in his homeland and be understood as one of many forms of sexual desire, though still an illness that begged to be cured.

Psychopathia Sexualis set the stage for subsequent work that attempted to characterize homosexuality from a clinical perspective. British psychologist Havelock Ellis, for example, took issue with Krafft-Ebing's conclusion that homosexuality was a degenerate malady and instead put forth the idea that it was a "congenital sexual inversion"—at least among the respected, well-bred classes. To Havelock, the lower classes and various close-quarter organizations such as the military inhabited environments that tolerated many vices including homosexuality, but he was at pains to explain its appearance in upper-class communities and institutions where moral standards dictated its condemnation. In his 1896 book *Sexual Inversion*, Ellis stated, "It requires a very strong impetus to go against this compact social force which, on every side, constrains the individual into the paths of heterosexual love. That impetus, in a well-bred individual who leads the normal life of his fellow men and who feels the ordinary degree of respect for the social feeling surrounding him, can only be supplied by a fundamental—usually, it is probable, inborn—perversion of the sexual instinct, rendering the individual organically abnormal." Thus, in Ellis's opinion, respectable persons who exhibited and acted on same-sex attraction when all polite society's disapproval weighed on their conscience must be directed by some inborn predisposition toward this deviance. In addition, Ellis argued that because so many great thinkers, artists, and statesmen were homosexual, it was incorrect to assume that their lives were immoral considering the contributions they made to society.

Famed psychologist Sigmund Freud was well versed with the conclusions of both Krafft-Ebing and Ellis when he addressed the subject of homosexuality. Freud agreed with Ellis that homosexuality was not a perverse condition. In an often-quoted letter written in 1935 to a concerned mother of a homosexual, Freud contended, "Homosexuality is assuredly no advantage, but it is nothing to be ashamed of, no vice, no degradation, it cannot be classified as an illness." Speaking for those who followed his novel theorizing, he continued, "We consider it to be a variation of the sexual function produced by a certain arrest of sexual development." This argument, however, veered sharply from Ellis's summations. Freud believed all people are born exhibiting bisexual traits and that only through parental and social influences—and perhaps some biological factors—do people conform to or stray from a sexual norm. Therefore, because heterosexual relationships are mandated as "normal" within society, homosexual inclinations are "abnormal" only insofar as they do not follow this path.

Though his reputation and works influenced much of psychology after him, Freud's analysis was certainly not the last word on the potential psychological explanations of homosexuality. Some found Freud's notion of inherent bisexuality to be improbable, while others continued to investigate homosexuality as pathology. Detractors of these psychological studies in general also pointed out that the analyses of Freud, Krafft-Ebing, and others were quite small and consisted mainly of men who were already seeking treatment for mental disorders. In 1957 University of California psychology professor Evelyn Hooker published the results of a more wide-ranging study that approached the subject of homosexuality from another angle. Instead of focusing on gay men who were in therapy, Hooker and her team sought out homosexual and heterosexual men that were well-functioning members of society and subjected them to a battery of psychological tests to determine if maladjustment could be clearly associated with homosexuality. The results of Hooker's exams showed that both homosexuals and heterosexuals exhibited the same degree of social adjustment, leaving researchers unable to determine a respondent's sexual orientation from his test results. Hooker's findings suggested that homosexuality could not be a pathological condition. In a 2003 brief, the American Psychological Association said of Hooker's results, "The fact that no differences were found between gay and straight participants sparked more research in this area and began to dismantle the myth that homosexual men and women are inherently unhealthy." It was not until 1973, however, that the American Psychiatric Association—swayed by Hooker's study and duplicate trials—removed homosexuality from the *Diagnostic and Statistical Manual of Mental Disorders*, the standard classification guide used by mental health professionals worldwide.

Since the declassification of homosexuality as a sociopathic disorder, biologists have become active in debating whether there may be a genetic predisposition for same-sex attraction. In the 1990s, Dean Hamer and colleagues working at the National Cancer Institute studied gay brothers and their families to determine if there could be a hereditary correlation. Using DNA analysis, Hamer discovered five genes in the maternally transferred X chromosome that reappeared in thirty-three of forty pairs of the siblings. Hamer was cautious in stating that his team's research suggested that the gene linkages corresponded to a homosexual predisposition. The media, however, trumpeted the publication of the 1993 report as the discovery of a "gay gene." Most ignored the fact that Hamer maintained his work only reinforced the notion that biology may be a factor in explaining homosexuality—and specifically homosexuality that is inherited maternally. When subsequent tests in the latter part of the decade failed to confirm Hamer's results, the controversy cooled.

In a January 2008 article for *Gay & Lesbian Review Worldwide*, neurobiologist Neena Schwartz of Northwestern University offered her opinion on the media and scientific interest in the "gay gene" theory and the desire to define a basis for homosexuality. She wrote:

> "Biology" as a causative agent can mean different things to different people: sex hormone levels in the adult; the hormones or other factors during early brain development of a fetus *in utero* or soon after birth; or the genes for some factor affecting the brain that's involved with gender identity. A behavior pattern as complex and variable as homosexuality cannot possibly be due to a single altered gene or even several genes alone.... On the other hand, homosexuality as a way of life is so compelling to so many gay people, including myself, that it seems unlikely to this biologist that it can be due wholly to social factors completely divorced from biology.

Although Schwartz ultimately laments the fact that no matter what scientific findings suggest, she lays bare the fact that the origins or causation of this "way of life" are still indistinct. Although no longer characterized as a sickness in scientific circles, researchers are still attempting to unravel the potential

role of genetics, the influence of hormones in fetal development, birth order, and other factors that may clarify homosexuality as a natural variant of sexual orientation. However,
as Schwartz points out, what society will make of those conclusions is uncertain and may beg the question of why so
much is invested in finding answers.

The first chapter of *Opposing Viewpoints: Homosexuality*
asks the question What Is the Basis of Homosexuality? A se-
lection of authors from differing backgrounds takes up this
seemingly fundamental query and provides insight into why
the answer may be important not simply to psychologists, biologists, and homosexuals but also to society at large. The remaining chapters in this book then expand on some of the
key interpretations of that first chapter and show how they
have come to shape public policy in the United States. In
chapters entitled Should Same-Sex Marriage Be Legal?, Should
Same-Sex Partners Be Allowed to Adopt?, and Should Homosexuals Be Excluded from Certain Organizations?, other observers and commentators bring to light the way in which the
courts, legislatures, and civic and private institutions have
contended with homosexuality as a stigma of degeneracy and
pathology is supplanted with promises of equal treatment and
equal rights. How the nation will negotiate this transition is
still unclear, but the variety of viewpoints within this anthol-
ogy attests to the fact that this issue and the debates that sur-
round it are forcing Americans to confront their beliefs, their
tolerances, and their values.

OPPOSING
VIEWPOINTS®
SERIES

CHAPTER 1

What Is the Basis of Homosexuality?

Chapter Preface

Conservapedia, a popular online resource written from an acknowledged conservative viewpoint, maintains, "The causes of homosexuality are attributable to man's sinful nature, nurture and environment, and personal choice." The author or authors of this entry stipulate that the degree to which these factors contribute to homosexuality remains unknown, but Conservapedia insists the contrasting, liberal argument that homosexuality is biologically determined is not supported by evidence. Instead, Conservapedia calls upon the "moral authority" of the Bible to suggest that deviance from God's laws—such as embracing homosexuality—is a personal choice affected, in part, by the environment in which an individual matures. To further this argument, the resource attests that "studies today have shown that religious upbringing and culture can strongly affect rates of homosexuality."

The Conservapedia entry clearly illustrates a persistent, if assumed, dichotomy in explaining the causes of homosexuality. Namely, homosexuality is characterized as either a fallen state brought on by choice and environment or as a biological imperative that is coded in the genes or hardwired in the process of fetal development. In fact, a 1991 study of gay twins suggested that there may be a genetic factor in sexual orientation, and other contemporary research into birth order and brain size offered congenital explanations. The inability of scientists to clearly repeat the findings of some of these studies, however, has cast doubt on pure biological determinism.

Today, many scientists and psychologists are reluctant to speak of a specific cause of homosexuality. Advocating the complexity and multifaceted nature of sexual orientation, a portion of those seeking to understand sexual orientation have supported the notion that homosexuality may be the result of a convergence of biological, environmental, social, and personal influences. The American Psychological Association, for example, attests, "No findings have emerged that permit scientists to conclude that sexual orientation is determined by any particular factor or factors. Many think that nature and nurture both play complex roles." At the same time, the organization contends that "most people experience little or no sense of choice about their sexual orientation." Other research, however, suggests that sexual orientation may be somewhat fluid, pointing to the fact that some people—typically women—are able to switch easily between heterosexual and homosexual relationships over the course of their lives.

In the following chapter, several commentators offer their views on the basis of homosexuality. Some contend that it is a condition brought on by choice or even moral failing, while others look to biological factors that might define homosexuality as an unalterable predisposition. Though continued research in this area indicates the significance of the pursuit, some observers are quick to note that sexual orientation is only a part of self-identity and that the desire to find a causative explanation may reveal more about society's motivations than any individual's need for an answer.

| "*Homosexuality is a congenital condition much like being 'left-handed.'*"

Homosexuals Are Born Gay

Dan Eden

In the following viewpoint, Dan Eden asserts that homosexuality is not determined by lifestyle choice but is instead a genetic condition shaped by early brain development. According to Eden, science has shown that changes in stress levels of pregnant mothers may inhibit the "defeminization" of male fetuses by interfering with the aggregation of testosterone in the brain's hypothalamus. He contends that a similar imbalance of hormones may explain lesbianism as well. Dan Eden is a staff writer for View-zone, an online journal that publishes stories on unusual science, mysterious history, conspiracy theories, and other cultural topics.

As you read, consider the following questions:

1. According to Eden, what section, or nuclei, of the hypothalamus is larger in volume in heterosexual men than in homosexual males and all females?

2. As Eden relates, if a mother experiences stress during the early stages of pregnancy, what hormone may "steal" the receptor sites in the brain usually occupied by testosterone?

3. As the author speculates, why might the fetal brain's vulnerability to stress not have been corrected through evolution?

Homosexuality effects from 8% to 15% of all males and slightly less for females. To put this in context, there are as many gays and lesbians in America today (2011) as there are unemployed citizens. Most carry the burden of hiding their sexual identity for fear of being disrespected or mistreated by the general population who remain ignorant to the causes and circumstances of homosexuality. This is puzzling in light of the plethora of investigative work that has been done on the phenomenon.

Ignoring the Research

In 1959 a report was published with the title "Organizing Action of Prenatally Administered Testosterone Propionate on the Tissues Mediating Mating Behavior in the Female Guinea Pig" by Charles H. Phoenix, Robert W. Goy, Arnold A. Gerall, and William C. Young. This was one of those "animal studies"—of interest only to psychologists and neurologists. In 1991, the popular journal, *Science*, published a paper that revisited the 1959 report and included many more recent studies. Their paper came to the conclusion:

> "This finding indicates that INAH [part of the hypothalamus] is dimorphic with sexual orientation, at least in men, and suggests that sexual orientation has a biological substrate."

Ever since *Science* published the article, I've been waiting for the big changes. But they have been slow. Public opinion still maintains that homosexuals have chosen to live a deviant lifestyle. Some of the worst hate towards homosexuals—from an anti-homosexual religious group that targets veterans' funerals—comes from the belief that it is a chosen lifestyle.

Ignorance about the cause of homosexuality has been responsible for many teen suicides as well as violence against teens who are perceived as different by their classmates. School officials, even parents of homosexual children, do little to clarify this condition and seem often to turn away from the issue altogether.

Many church leaders continue to equate homosexuality as a sin, suggesting that through prayer they could be "made whole." The husband of one of the top Republican presidential candidates [referring to Michele Bachmann] runs a clinic, claiming to be able to "cure" homosexuality as if it were merely a bad decision. This view is echoed in many religious churches, based on the writings of the apostle Paul:

> "Do not be deceived: Neither the sexually immoral nor idolaters nor adulterers nor male prostitutes nor homosexual offenders nor thieves nor the greedy nor drunkards nor slanderers nor swindlers will inherit the kingdom of God. And that is what some of you were. But you were washed, you were sanctified, you were justified in the name of the Lord Jesus Christ and by the Spirit of our God."—I Corinthians 6:9–11 [New International Version]

What's going on here? Can homosexuality be "washed away" with conservative beliefs?

Homosexuality Is a Congenital Condition

The Conservapedia [an online resource written from a conservative point of view] states that:

> "The causes of homosexuality are attributable to man's sinful nature, nurture and environment, and personal choice."

But scientific research directly contradicts this.

Homosexuality is a congenital condition much like being "left-handed." Before you dismiss the analogy remember there were times in history when being left-handed (the archaic meaning of "sinister") meant you were possessed by evil. You could have been hanged, burned, stoned to death or buried alive. Having personally lived in an Arab country, I can assure you that being left-handed was something that I did my best to hide. Today we know that left-handedness is the result of excess testosterone slowing the growth of the left hemisphere in the developing fetal brain. It's not a choice, it's a condition.

Ironically, homosexuality is caused much the same way as being left-handed. Instead of excess testosterone, the developing male fetus receives too little, often too late.

Researchers naturally focus on an organ in the brain called the *hypothalamus* because it is known to be responsible for gender preference. It is also what is called *dimorphic*, meaning its structure is different in males and females. There's also differences in the hypothalamus between homosexuals and heterosexuals. Recent studies of the different sections or *nuclei* have revealed much that was not known before. And there have also been some surprises.

With advances in laboratory technology, a specific region of the hypothalamus, called the sexually dimorphic nucleus (SDN), has been the focus of some interesting research. The SDN is the most conspicuous anatomical male/female difference in the mammalian brain. The nucleus is 3 to 8 times larger in males than in females. Another nucleus of the hypothalamus, INAH 3, reveals that heterosexual males have double the volume of both homosexual and female subjects.

[According to the 1991 *Science* article,]

"As has been reported previously, INAH 3 was more than twice as large in the heterosexual men as in the women. It was also, however, more than twice as large as in the homosexual men."

A review of current research shows that there is no evidence supporting a social cause for homosexuality. On the

Research on Biological Indicators of Homosexuality

A host of biological indicators of homosexuality boost the theory [of biology's influence on sexual orientation]. For example, research from the University of Liverpool in England has shown that gay men and lesbians are more likely than straights to be left-handed and that lesbians have hand patterns that resemble a man's more than a straight female's. Dennis McFadden, a scientist at the University of Texas at Austin, has reported that lesbians' auditory systems seem to develop somewhere between what is typical for heterosexual men and women. According to studies done by Marc Breedlove, a psychologist at the University of California, Berkeley, there is a direct correlation between the lengths of some fingers of the hand and gayness.

Mubarak Dahir, "Why Are We Gay?,"
Advocate, July 17, 2001.

contrary, there are multiple studies, both with animals and humans, demonstrating the causative relationship with the prenatal testosterone during a critical stage in "defeminization."

Dr. Harry Harlow's famous studies with rhesus monkeys demonstrated that such things as love and the ability to nurture healthy children was a learned skill that could be altered by after-birth experiences. This non-biologic effect may play a role in female homosexuality and may also be a contributing factor in the degree to which congenital homosexuality is either expressed or repressed. But they do not cause homosexuality.

Gendering Brains

Embryology teaches that early embryos all start out as female. At some point in early gestation, if the chromosomes destine the fetus to be male, the embryo is altered by the genetically programmed addition of certain hormones, called androgens. These androgens, especially testosterone, instruct the embryo to develop male characteristics. In their absence, the embryo continues to develop into a female.

An "XX" pair of chromosomes will yield a female; an "XY" pair will result in a male. The "X" is always contributed from the mother (since she has only "X's"), but the father can contribute either an "X" or a "Y"—so it is the father's genetic contribution that determines the gender of the child. If homosexual men have "XY" pairs which are typically male in all respects, what makes their hypothalamus different?

In a paper published almost a quarter of a century ago, a research psychologist at Villanova University was also puzzled about gender. Dr. Ingeborg Ward was studying the sexual behavior of rats, years before the role of the hypothalamus was even suspected of gendering human brains.

Dr. Ward divided some pregnant rats into three groups. Suspecting that something special might be happening in the early stages of pregnancy, she subjected the first group to stress during the first ten days of gestation by irritating the mother rats with bright lights, noise and annoying vibrations. Ten days in a rat's pregnancy corresponds to the first trimester (3 months) of a human pregnancy. The second group was subjected to stress towards the end of their pregnancy, just before birth. The third group was comprised of male offspring from both prenatal stressed mothers and unstressed mothers. These babies were subjected to the same stress-producing stimuli.

Dr. Ward then allowed all the males to grow to adulthood without further interference. She then placed each group of males in cages with healthy females to observe their ability and desire to mate with normal adult females. Here is what happened:

"Abstract: Male rats were exposed to prenatal (i.e., before they were born) or postnatal (after they were born) stress, or both. The prenatally stressed males showed low levels of male copulatory behavior and high rates of female lordotic responding (i.e., "lordotic" refers to mounting behavior which usually occurs during mating). Postnatal stress had no effect. The modifications are attributed to stress-mediated alterations in the ratio of adrenal to gonadal androgens during critical stages of sexual differentiation. Specifically, it appears that stress causes an increase in the weak adrenal androgen, androstenedione, from the maternal fetal adrenal cortices, or both, and a concurrent decrease in the potent gonadal androgen, testosterone."

If the baby carries "XY" chromosomes and is destined to become a male, testosterone needs to activate the newly forming hypothalamus. This is the first known critical phase of "defeminization" when something can go awry, upsetting the master plan.

If a mother is stressed during the early stages of pregnancy, she will release an adrenaline-related hormone into her shared bloodstream with her unborn baby. This hormone, called androstenedione, is structurally similar to testosterone, the male hormone. Both are androgens, but testosterone is more than twenty times as potent as androstenedione.

It has also recently been suggested that testosterone actually breaks down to estradiol in some way that androstenedione may not, further implicating this androgen in disrupting the process of early brain development.

Inhibitors to Defeminization in Males

Because the stress hormone seems to mimic testosterone, there is the delay or blockage of the effectiveness of testosterone, even if it is plentiful. This causes a disturbance in the "defeminization" of the hypothalamus.

In 1972, Dr. Ward had no idea that androstenedione in male pregnancies would prevent or inhibit the hypothalamus to develop into a healthy male brain, but this stress-related hormone now appears to do just that. The brain makes its gender commitment very early in development and, once committed to either male or female, it cannot change.

The interference with environmental testosterone in the later stages of pregnancy does little or nothing to inhibit gender development of the body. By mid-pregnancy, the gonads can produce enough systemic testosterone to develop the body along male plans; however, problems do happen in these later stages. Sometimes the receptors which receive testosterone are defective or greatly reduced in number. This is generally seen as a defect resulting from the initial blocking of testosterone by the presence of other androgens. This can inhibit the effectiveness of testosterone and cause a less effective defeminization.

In Dr. Ward's own words:

"... The present data support the hypothesis that exposure of pregnant rats to environmental stressors modifies the normal process of sexual behavior differentiation in male fetuses by decreasing functional testosterone and elevating androstenedione levels during prenatal development. During stress conditions, plasma testosterone emanating from the gonads decreases while adrenal androstenedione rises. The molecular structure of the two androgens, being very similar, it is postulated that the two hormones compete for the same receptor sites. Since androstenedione is a less potent androgen than testosterone, the decrease in male copulatory ability and increased lordotic potential seen in the prenatally stressed animals of the present study would be expected. The relative difference in potency between testosterone and androstenedione has been repeatedly demonstrated.

Homosexuality as a Form of Population Control

As we begin to understand that homosexuality is not inherited, we note that it occurs in more or less the same frequency of the population. This could suggest that a preference for one's own gender served some evolutionary benefit. If not, we should expect the perceived vulnerability of the developing fetal brain to have been corrected. But what could the benefit be?

Again, in Dr. Ward's own words:

> "The resulting alterations in sexual behavior provide the basis for an effective population control mechanism, since offspring so affected would not possess the behavioral repertoire necessary to contribute to population growth. Thus, the environment, by triggering an adrenal stress response, may control the reproductive capacity of successive generations of differentiating fetuses and, thereby, population size."

Lesbians May Experience the Same Hormone Reaction

The developing female fetus is expecting no prenatal testosterone. This molecule is significant only if the fetus is destined to be male. Androstenedione, produced by maternal stress, closely resembles testosterone. Even a small amount of this molecule during the critical first trimester of pregnancy could be enough to make the developing hypothalamus defeminized or masculine. So the same mechanism can possibly explain both male and female homosexuality.

"The sheer number of exceptions to the 'born gay' theory should be a warning to researchers and media to proceed with caution before declaring that science has 'proved' that homosexuality is genetic."

Born or Bred?
Science Does Not Support
the Claim That Homosexuality
Is Genetic

Robert H. Knight

Robert H. Knight is director of the Culture and Family Institute, an affiliate of Concerned Women for America, a national organization determined to bring biblical principles into the shaping of public policy. This viewpoint is a revised and updated version of "Born & Bred: The Debate Over the Cause of Homosexuality" (last updated in June 2000) by former Concerned Women of America staff writer Trudy Chun. In the following viewpoint, Knight questions or refutes the findings of several research studies that some advocates and media outlets have used to support the notion that homosexuality is a genetic trait. According to Knight, careful examination of the literature often reveals that these studies do not claim that they provide conclusive proof of a link between genes and homosexuality. Instead, many of the researchers point out that behaviors and preferences are influenced by a host of factors including learned social patterns and environment. Knight believes it is wrong to push the "gay gene" theory because it robs people of the choice they might have in shaping their own sexual identity.

As you read, consider the following questions:

1. As Knight writes, what did Simon LeVay state were some of the shortcomings of his own study of the hypothalamus and its relation to sexual orientation?

2. According to Knight, why did Jeffrey Satinover argue that Bailey and Pillard's twins study failed to show that homosexuality was genetically determined?

3. According to Satinover, why is it important to distinguish between correlation and causation?

The debate over homosexual "marriage" often becomes focused on whether homosexuality is a learned behavior or a genetic trait. Many homosexual activists insist that "science" has shown that homosexuality is inborn, cannot be changed, and that therefore they should have the "right to marry" each other.

Beginning in the early 1990s, activists began arguing that scientific research has proven that homosexuality has a genetic or hormonal cause. A handful of studies, none of them replicated and all exposed as methodologically unsound or misrepresented, have linked sexual orientation to everything from differences in portions of the brain,[1, 2] to genes,[3] finger length,[4] inner ear differences,[5] eye blinking,[6] and "neuro-hormonal differentiation."[7]

Meanwhile, Columbia University professor of psychiatry Dr. Robert Spitzer, who was instrumental in removing homosexuality in 1973 from the American Psychiatric Association's list of mental disorders, wrote a study published in the October 2003 *Archives of Sexual Behavior*. He contended that people can change their "sexual orientation" from homosexual to heterosexual.[8] Spitzer interviewed more than 200 people, most of whom claimed that through reparative therapy counseling, their desires for same-sex partners either diminished significantly or they changed over to heterosexual orientation. Although still a proponent of homosexual activism, Spitzer has been attacked unmercifully by former admirers for this breach of the ideology that people are "born gay and can't change." Immutability is a central tenet of demands for "gay rights" and "gay marriage."

---

[1] D.F. Swaab and M.A. Hofman, *Brain Res.* 537 (1990): 141–48, as cited in Dennis McFadden and E.G. Pasanen, "Comparisons of the auditory systems of heterosexuals and homosexuals: Click-evoked otoacoustic emissions," *Proceedings of the National. Academy of Science USA* 95 (March 1998): 709–13.

[2] Simon LeVay, "A Difference in Hypothalamic Structure Between Heterosexual and Homosexual Men," *Science* Vol. 253 (1991): 1034–37.

[3] D.H. Hamer, S. Hu, V.L. Magnuson, N. Hu and A.M.L. Pattatucci, *Science* 261(1993): 321–27, as cited in McFadden.

[4] B.J. Sigesmund, "Let Your Fingers Do the Talking," *Newsweek* "Web Exclusive," 31 March 2000.

[5] McFadden and Pasanen.

[6] "Sexual orientation 'hard-wired' before birth—startling new evidence revealed in the blink of an eye," press release, University of East London (UEL), England, October 2, 2003, reporting on findings by the UEL's Dr. Qazi Rahman, along with the Institute of Psychiatry's Dr. Veena Kumari and Dr. Glenn Wilson. In terms of eye-blink reactions to sudden loud noises, "The team discovered significant differences in the response between male and female, and heterosexual and homosexual subjects." Rahman: "The startle response is pre-conscious and cannot be learned."

[7] Qazi Rahman, "Comments on the Neuroanatomy of Human Sexual Orientation and Proposed Neuroendocrine Hypotheses," *Contemporary Neurology* (1999): Number 2A: http://mitpress.mit.edu/jrnls-catalog/cont-neuro.html.

[8] Robert L. Spitzer, "Can Some Gay Men and Lesbians Change Their Sexual Orientation?", *Archives of Sexual Behavior*, Vol. 32, No. 5, October 2003: 403–417.

Because no single study can be regarded as definitive, more research on people who have overcome homosexuality needs to be done. But a considerable body of previous literature about change from homosexuality to heterosexuality has been compiled, and the sheer number of exceptions to the "born gay" theory should be a warning to researchers and media to proceed with caution before declaring that science has "proved" that homosexuality is genetic.[9]

Other recent developments also suggest that homosexuality is not genetically determined. The *Washington Post* reported that bisexuality is fashionable among many young teen girls, who go back and forth from being "straight" to "gay" to "bi" to "straight" again.[10]

Post reporter Laura Sessions Stepp writes:

> Recent studies among women suggest that female homosexuality may be grounded more in social interaction, may present itself as an emotional attraction in addition to or in place of a physical one, and may change over time.[11]

She cites one such study by Lisa M. Diamond, assistant professor of psychology and gender studies at the University of Utah, who in 1994 began studying a group of females aged 16 to 23 who were attracted to other females.[12] Over the course of the study, "almost two-thirds have changed labels," Stepp reports.

Against increasing evidence that homosexual behavior is neither inevitable nor impossible to resist, a number of studies have been widely publicized as "proof" of a genetic

---

[9] See, for instance, Charles Socarides, *A Freedom Too Far: A Psychoanalyst Answers 1,000 Questions About Causes and Cure and the Impact of the Gay Rights Movement on American Society* (Phoenix, Arizona: Adam Margrave Books, 1996), pp. 115–155, particularly pp. 151–152.

[10] Laura Sessions Stepp, "Partway Gay? For Some Teen Girls, Sexual Preference Is a Shifting Concept," *The Washington Post*, January 4, 2004, p. D-1.

[11] Ibid.

[12] Lisa M. Diamond, "Was it a phase? Young women's relinquishment of lesbian/bisexual identities over a 5-year period," *Journal of Personality & Social Psychology* (in press as of 2004).

component. But they are either poorly constructed or misreported as to their significance.

In 1993, Columbia University psychiatry professors Drs. William Byne and Bruce Parsons examined the most prominent "gay gene" studies on brain structure and on identical twins, and published the results in the *Archives of General Psychiatry*. They found numerous methodological flaws in all of the studies, and concluded that:

> There is no evidence at present to substantiate a biologic theory. . . . [T]he appeal of current biologic explanations for sexual orientation may derive more from dissatisfaction with the present status of psychosocial explanations than from a substantiating body of experimental data.[13]

After he was roundly attacked by homosexual activists, who accused him of providing ammunition for conservatives to challenge the gay rights/civil rights comparison based on immutability, Byne . . . stated that he was also skeptical of environmental theories of sexual orientation. He wrote: "There is no compelling evidence to support any singular psychosocial explanation," and that he would never "imply that one consciously decides one's sexual orientation."[14] But the fact remains that Dr. Byne has poked gaping holes in the most influential studies purporting to prove that homosexuality is inborn.

In May 2000, the American Psychiatric Association issued a Fact Sheet, "Gay, Lesbian and Bisexual Issues," which includes this statement:

> "Currently, there is a renewed interest in searching for biological etiologies for homosexuality. However, to date there

[13] William Byne and Bruce Parsons, "Human Sexual Orientation: The Biologic Theories Reappraised," *Archives of General Psychiatry*, Vol. 50, March 1993: 228–239.

[14] Letter from William Byne to Dean Hamer, 2 July 1993, as quoted in Chandler Burr, *A Separate Creation: The Search for the Biological Origins of Sexual Orientation* (New York, New York: Hyperion, 1996), p. 81.

are no replicated scientific studies supporting any specific biological etiology for homosexuality."

Beyond the false comfort that homosexuals need not seek to alter their behavior in any way, there may be another motive behind the release and enthusiastic reporting of these studies: political advantage. As Natalie Angier wrote in the *New York Times* on September 1, 1991:

> [P]roof of an inborn difference between gay and heterosexual men could provide further ammunition in the battle against discrimination. If homosexuality were viewed legally as a biological phenomenon, rather than a fuzzier matter of "choice" or "preference," then gay people could no more rightfully be kept out of the military, a housing complex or a teaching job than could, say blacks.[15]

Simon LeVay, whose brain study in 1991 "jumped from the pages of the periodical *Science* to the *New York Times* and *Time*, then to CNN and *Nightline*, and from there to the dinner tables and offices of the country," according to writer Chandler Burr, was quite open in his assessment of the possible impact of his work. "[P]eople who think gays and lesbians are born that way are also more likely to support gay rights."[16]

In his book *Homosexuality and the Politics of Truth*, Dr. Jeffrey Satinover writes:

> We will see later the falsity of activists' repeated assertions that homosexuality is immutable. They seek to create the impression that *science* has settled these questions, but it most certainly has not. Instead, the changes that have oc-

---

[15] Natalie Angier, quoted in Charles W. Socarides, "A Freedom Too Far," (Phoenix, Arizona: Adam Margrave Books, 1995), p. 94.

[16] Simon LeVay, quoted in A. Dean Byrd, Ph.D., Shirley E. Cox, Ph.D., and Jeffrey W. Robinson, Ph.D., "The Innate-Immutable Argument Finds No Basis in Science," 2002, the National Association for the Research and Therapy of Homosexuality, http://www.narth.com/docs/innate.html.

curred in both public and professional opinion have resulted from politics, pressure, and public relations.[17]

Despite critical examination, as well as comments by the studies' own authors that the "gay" research has been distorted or exaggerated, some of the studies are often cited as "proof" that "gays are born that way." A few other studies have arisen in more recent years with as many flaws or have been misreported in similar fashion. Here is a brief overview of some of the studies:

UCLA's Study on Genes and Mice Brains

In October 2003, the journal *Molecular Brain Research* published a study by UCLA researchers indicating that sexual identity is genetic.[18] Reuters reported it this way: "Sexual identity is wired into the genes, which discounts the concept that homosexuality and transgender sexuality are a choice, California researchers reported."[19] A number of other media outlets picked up on this theme, creating the impression that this study was yet one more piece of evidence for a genetic theory of homosexuality.

The trouble is, the study doesn't say anything about homosexuality. All it does is support a widely accepted theory about hormones and gender. Here is Princeton professor Dr. Jeffrey Satinover's assessment:

> The research is a decent piece of basic science and confirms what geneticists have long known must be the case: That the hormonal milieu that causes sexual differentiation between males and females is itself determined by genes, in mice as in men. This comes as no surprise.

---

[17] Jeffrey Satinover, M.D., *Homosexuality and the Politics of Truth* (Grand Rapids, Michigan: Hamewith Books, Baker Books, 1996), p. 38.

[18] Phoebe Dewing, Tao Shi, Steve Horvath and Eric Vilain, "Sexually dimorphic gene expression in mouse brain precedes gonadal differentiation," *Molecular Brain Research*, Vol. 118, Issues 1-2, 21 October 2003: 82–90.

[19] Reuters, "Study says sexual identity is genetic," 20 October 2003.

But this research says absolutely nothing about homosexuality or transsexualism and any who claim it does are either ill-informed about genetics, or if not, are deliberately abusing their scientific knowledge and or credentials in the service of politics in precisely the same way that Soviet-era geneticists such as Lysenko did—either in the naïve hope that distortion of the truth can produce a better society or out of fear for their career prospects. In either case they should be roundly rebuked for doing so.[20]

The Hypothalamus

The first widely publicized claim for a "gay gene" came in 1991 when Salk Institute researcher Dr. Simon LeVay published a study in the journal *Science* noting a difference in a brain structure called the hypothalamus when evaluating 35 men—19 homosexuals and 16 heterosexuals.[21] LeVay found that the hypothalamus was generally larger in heterosexual men than in homosexual men. He concluded that the findings "suggest that sexual orientation has a biologic substrate."[22]

The media splashed the study on front pages and TV and radio broadcasts from coast to coast, despite the fact that LeVay himself cautioned:

"It's important to stress what I didn't find. I did not prove that homosexuality is genetic, or find a genetic cause for being gay. I didn't show that gay men are born that way, the most common mistake people make in interpreting my work. Nor did I locate a gay center in the brain.... Since I looked at adult brains, we don't know if the differences I found were there at birth, or if they appeared later."[23]

---

[20] E-mail correspondence, 21 October 2003.

[21] LeVay, op cit.

[22] Ibid.

[23] Quoted in David Nimmons, "Sex and the Brain," *Discover*, Vol. 5, No. 3 (March 1994): 64–71 and cited in A. Dean Byrd, Ph.D., Shirley E. Cox, Ph.D., and Jeffrey W. Robinson, Ph.D., "The Innate-Immutable Argument Finds No Basis in Science," National Association of Research and Therapy for Homosexuality Web site, http://www.narth.com/docs/innate.html, downloaded 12 January 2004.

The study also had major problems, which LeVay himself readily admits. First, all 19 of his homosexual subjects died of complications associated with AIDS. The difference in the hypothalamus might have been caused by chemical changes in the brain as a response to AIDS.

Dr. Byne argued in *Scientific American* that "[LeVay's] inclusion of a few brains from heterosexual men with AIDS did not adequately address the fact that at the time of death virtually all men with AIDS have decreased testosterone levels as the result of the disease itself or the side effects of particular treatments.... Thus it is possible that the effects on the size of the INAH 3 [hypothalamus] that he attributed to sexual orientation were actually caused by the hormonal abnormalities associated with AIDS."[24]

In addition, six of the "heterosexual" men died of AIDS. LeVay admitted later that he didn't actually know whether the subjects in his heterosexual sample were, indeed, heterosexual; all of these subjects were simply "presumed heterosexual." Given that very few straight men in San Francisco were contracting AIDS at the time (and still aren't), this was a wildly unscientific assumption.

Another weakness of LeVay's study is that his sample included major "exceptions." Three of the homosexuals had larger clusters of neurons than the mean size for the heterosexuals, and three of the heterosexuals had clusters smaller than the mean size for the homosexuals. LeVay acknowledged that these exceptions "hint at the possibility that sexual orientation, although an important variable, may not be the sole determinant of INAH 3 [hypothalamus] size."[25]

LeVay is an open homosexual, and some comments he made to *Newsweek* suggest he had an agenda from the outset of the research. He said he believes that America must be convinced that homosexuality is biologically determined. "It's im-

[24] E. Byne, "The Biological Evidence Challenged," *Scientific American* (May 1994): 50–5.
[25] LeVay.

portant to educate society," he said. "I think this issue does affect religious and legal attitudes."[26]

Since LeVay released his study, other researchers have found that life experiences can alter brain structures, so it is premature to assume inborn origins for behavioral differences. In 1997, for example, University of California at Berkeley psychologist Marc Breedlove released a study that showed that sexual activities of rats actually changed structural aspects of the brain at the base of the spinal cord. Breedlove said:

> These findings give us proof for what we theoretically know to be the case—that sexual experience can alter the structure of the brain, just as genes can alter it. You can't assume that because you find a structural difference in the brain, that it was caused by genes. You don't know how it got there.[27]

Breedlove is not an activist out to prove homosexuality is not biological. In fact, he said he believes that a genetic component exists somewhere and is doing his own research in this area.

The X Chromosome

In 1993, a group of medical researchers at the National Cancer Institute (NCI) led by Dr. Dean H. Hamer released a study of 40 pairs of brothers that linked homosexuality to the X chromosome. The research, published in *Science*, reported that 33 of the pairs of brothers had DNA markers in the chromosome region known as Xq28.

The study won an enormous amount of media attention, and Hamer's own activities as a homosexual activist within NCI were ignored when Hamer offered interviews only when reporters agreed not to identify him as a homosexual.

[26] D. Gelman, D. Foote, T. Barrett, M. Talbot, "Born or Bred," *Newsweek*, 24 February 1992, 46–53.

[27] Pat McBroom, "Sexual Experience May Affect Brain Structure," *Berkeleyan* campus newspaper (University of California at Berkeley), 19 November 1997 (http://www.urel.berkeley.edu/berkeleyan/1997/1119/sexexp.html).

But even Hamer tempered his enthusiasm about the research results.

> We knew that the genes were only part of the answer," he said in a speech given in Salt Lake City. "We assumed the environment also played a role in sexual orientation, as it does in most, if not all behaviors.[28]

In a later interview, Hamer said, "Homosexuality is not purely genetic. . . . [E]nvironmental factors play a role. There is not a single master gene that makes people gay. . . . I don't think we will ever be able to predict who will be gay."[29]

Hamer's results are often misunderstood. Many believe that the study found an identical sequence (Xq28) on the X chromosome of all homosexual brothers in the study. In reality, what it found was matching sequences in each set of brothers who were both homosexual. Dr. Byne argues that in order to prove anything by this study, Hamer would have had to examine the Xq28 sequence of homosexual men's heterosexual brothers. Hamer insisted that such an inclusion would have confounded his study. Byne responds: "In other words, inclusion of heterosexual brothers might have revealed that something other than genes is responsible for sexual orientation."[30]

In the same edition of *Science* that carried the Hamer study, Elliot Gershon, chief of the clinical neurogenetics branch of the National Institute of Mental Health, said, "There's almost no finding that would be convincing by itself in this field. We really have to see an independent replication."[31]

---

[28] Dean Hamer, *The Science of Desire* (New York, New York: Simon & Schuster, 1994), p. 82.

[29] From speech in Salt Lake City in Lili Wright, "Science of Desire Is Topic for 'Gay Gene' Finder," *Salt Lake Tribune*, 28 April 1995.

[30] Byne.

[31] "Evidence for Homosexuality Gene," *Science*, Vol. 261, 16 July 1993: 291.

The National Cancer Institute sponsored the "gay gene" research. This study alone cost $419,000 of the institute's taxpayer-backed funds, according to the *Washington Times*.[32]

The National Institutes of Health's Office of Research Integrity investigated Hamer over allegations by a colleague that he ignored evidence that conflicted with his hypothesis. NIH never released the results of the inquiry, but Hamer was shortly thereafter transferred to another section. He had done the "gay gene" research under a grant to work on Kaposi's sarcoma, a skin cancer that inordinately afflicts homosexual men.

One of Hamer's researchers told the *Times* that homosexuality is "not the only thing we study," but it is "a primary focus of study." Hamer reportedly stated he has pushed for an Office of Gay and Lesbian Health inside the National Institutes of Health, and he testified in opposition to Colorado's Amendment 2, which sought to keep homosexual activists from winning minority class status. Then-Sen. Robert C. Smith (R-New Hampshire) accused the doctor of "actively pursu[ing] . . . a gay agenda."[33]

Another fact that casts doubt on Hamer's conclusions is that other researchers tried to replicate his study but failed. In 1999, Drs. George Rice, Neil Risch and George Ebers published their findings in *Science* after attempting to replicate Hamer's Xq28 study. Their conclusion: "We were not able to confirm evidence for an Xq28-linked locus underlying male homosexuality." Moreover, they added that when another group of researchers (Sanders, et al.) tried to replicate Hamer's study, they too failed to find a genetic connection to homosexuality.[34]

---

[32] Joyce Price, "Federal Cancer Lab Hunts for Gay Gene," *The Washington Times*, 3 April 1994.

[33] Ibid.

[34] Dean H. Hamer, George Rice, Neil Risch, and George Ebers, et al. "Genetics and Male Sexual Orientation" (Technical Comment), *Science* 285 (6 August 1999): 803a.

The Twins Study

In 1991, J. Michael Bailey and Richard C. Pillard published a study that examined identical and fraternal twin brothers and adopted brothers in an effort to establish a genetic link to homosexuality. Fifty-two percent of the identical twins were reportedly homosexual, while only 22 percent of fraternal twins fell into the same category. But since identical twins have identical genetic material, the fact that nearly half of the identical twins were heterosexual effectively refutes the idea that homosexuality has a genetic basis.[35]

"This finding alone argues for the enormous importance of *nongenetic* factors influencing homosexuality," writes Dr. Jeffrey Satinover, "because . . . in order for something to be genetically *determined*, as opposed to merely influenced, the genetic heritability would need to approach 100 percent."[36] Satinover, a psychiatrist, notes that "*identical* twins reared together share more significant environmental influences than *nonidentical* twins reared together," and that narcissism, a key component of homosexuality, is more likely among identical twins who "grow up with mirror images of themselves."[37] (Italics in original.)

In his analysis of the medical evidence purportedly supporting a biological cause of homosexuality, Dr. Byne noted other twin studies:

> Without knowing what developmental experiences contribute to sexual orientation . . . the effects of common genes and common environments are difficult to disentangle. Resolving this issue requires studies of twins raised apart.[38]

---

[35] J. Michael Bailey, Richard C. Pillard, "A Genetic Study of Male Sexual Orientation," *Archives of General Psychiatry* 48 (1991): 108–96.

[36] Satinover, *Homosexuality and the Politics of Truth*, p. 85.

[37] Ibid.

[38] Byne.

Other physicians have also criticized the study for over-valuing the genetic influence.[39]

Dr. Byne's arguments might lead some activists to label him a "homophobe." He is, in reality, quite the contrary. Byne readily advocates societal acceptance of homosexuality and "gay rights," but nevertheless concludes, "Most of the links in the chain of reasoning from biology to social policy [regarding homosexuality], do not hold up under scrutiny."[40]

Bailey conducted another study in 1999, published in the March 2000 issue of the *Journal of Personality and Social Psychology*, which actually showed less possible genetic influence on homosexuality than the first twins study. He sent a questionnaire to the entire Australian Twin Registry. Only three pairs of identical male twins were both homosexual out of a total of 27 in which at least one was homosexual. Of the 16 fraternal male twins, none of the pairs were both homosexual. Bailey found similar results for lesbians.[41]

Hormones

In 1998, Dennis McFadden and Edward G. Pasanen published a study that evaluated auditory systems. Specifically, the study considered differences in echo-like waveforms emitted from an inner ear structure of people with normal hearing. These waves are higher in women than in men, a factor often attributed to the level of a person's exposure to androgen (a male hormone) in his or her early development as a fetus.[42]

In self-acknowledged lesbians, the waveforms ranged between those of men and those of heterosexual women. The researchers concluded that this suggests that female homosexuality could result from larger exposure to the male hormone

[39] T. Lidz, "A Reply to 'A Genetic Study of Male Sexual Orientation'" (letter), *Archives of General Psychiatry* 50 (1993): 240.
[40] Ibid.
[41] Stanton L. Jones, "The Incredibly Shrinking Gay Gene," *Christianity Today*, 4 October 1999, p. 53.
[42] McFadden.

androgen in the womb (homosexual men did not show the same variation).[43]

The media eagerly jumped on this bandwagon. But even the researchers themselves did not draw definitive conclusions. In the published study, they pointed out that exposure to "intense sounds, certain drugs, and other manipulations" can lower the level of these auditory waveforms. "Thus, it may be that something in the lifestyles of homosexual and bisexual females leads them to be exposed to one or more agents that have reduced the [waveforms], either temporarily or permanently."[44]

Moreover, even if the hearing differences were caused by an increased exposure to androgen in the womb, scientists would still be far from proving that this exposure is a cause of homosexuality—especially since the difference was not apparent in the male homosexual sample.

Finger Length

In March 2000, the media publicized a finger length study that indicated that lesbians had longer fingers than other women, perhaps because of greater exposure in the womb to androgen.

Typically, both sexes' index finger is slightly shorter than the ring finger—a difference that is seen more clearly on the right hand. In females, the ring finger and index finger are almost the same size, but in men the index finger is more noticeably shorter.

In this study, Berkeley's Dr. Breedlove, who had in 1997 shown how sexual activity can change brain structure, found that homosexual women's finger length had a tendency to follow the male pattern. But Breedlove cautioned about reading too much into the finding:

[43] Ibid, 2709.
[44] Ibid, 2712.

"There is no gene that forces a person to be straight or gay," he told CNN. ". . . I believe there are many social and psychological, as well as biological, factors that make up sexual preference."[45]

Dr. Jeffrey Satinover commented as follows on the study:

A girl who develops before and into puberty with a "masculinized habitus" (the result of excess maternal intrauterine androgen stimulated by a genetic condition in the fetus)—a stocky physique, facial hair, powerful muscles, a square jaw and long fingers—may suffer so much teasing and rejection by family and peers that she comes to think of herself as "not feminine" and so will seek solace in the arms of women. Indeed, this is an all-too-common pattern in the lives of "lesbians" and illustrates exactly how a strong genetic "association" can imply literally zero genetic causation whatsoever. It's rather remarkable that the authors failed to remark on the support their study provided not for any genetic association with lesbianism, but rather for the genetic association to secondary sexual expression in *homo sapiens* that Vilain et al. were only able to demonstrate in *mus musculus*. The attention paid to homosexuality in both cases, while ignoring straighforward sex, reflects the distinctly Orwellian effect that political correctness has on science: We now treat the differences between male and female as socially constructed and those between heterosexuality and homosexuality as innate and genetic.[46]

Eye Blinking

In October 2003, a team of English researchers announced that they had found "powerful new evidence that sexual orientation is 'hardwired' in the human brain before birth."[47]

---

[45] "Male hormone levels in womb may affect sexual orientation, study says," CNN.com, health, 29 March 2000, (http://www.cnn.com/2000/HEALTH/03/29/gay.fingers/index.html).

[46] Private communication with the author.

[47] "Sexual Orientation 'hard-wired' before birth—startling new evidence revealed in the blink of an eye," press release, University of East London, England, 2 October 2003.

Dr. Qazi Rahman of the University of East London and Dr. Veena Kumari and Dr. Glenn Wilson of the Institute of Psychiatry said they found sex differences in the startle response—the eye blink in response to loud noises.[48]

The authors found that women had a lesser "prepulse inhibition of the human startle response (PPI),"[49] that is, they blinked more readily than men, and that lesbians blinked less readily than other women. They used small samples, and, more significantly, found no difference between homosexual men and heterosexual men. Yet they gave the impression that their findings indicated that homosexuality is a pre-born condition.

"Because the startle response is known to be involuntary rather than learned, this strongly indicates that sexual orientation is largely determined before birth," said a press release from the University of East London.[50]

Dr. Rahman said in the release, "These findings may well affect the way we as a society deal with sexuality and the issues surrounding sexual orientation."

But the researchers themselves introduce some cautionary notes in the study:

> Although prenatal factors may be possible precursors to the neurobehavioral profiles observed in lesbians and gay men, whether neural differences underlie sexual orientation per se, or are a consequence of homosexual or heterosexual behavior, is yet to be determined.[51]

They also write: "Neuroanatomical and neurophysiological variations between heterosexuals and homosexuals may be due either to biological factors or to the influence of learning."[52]

---

[48] Qazi Rahman, Veena Kumari, and Glenn D. Wilson, "Sexual Orientation-Related Differences in Prepulse Inhibition of the Human Startle Response," *Behavioral Neuroscience*, Vol. 117 (5): 1096–1102.

[49] Ibid, p. 1096.

[50] Press release, "Sexual orientation 'hard-wired' before birth."

[51] Ibid., p. 1097.

[52] Ibid., p. 1099.

The team concluded that: "Our results show, for the first time, that PPI relates to sexual orientation and that homosexual women show a robust cross-sex shift. Homosexual women showed a masculinized PPI that was no different from that of heterosexual men. . . . Homosexual men did not differ from heterosexual men."[53]

Dr. Halstead Harrison, an associate professor emeritus in the Atmospheric Sciences Department of the University of Washington, reviewed the study, noted the small sizes of the test groups (14 lesbians and 15 heterosexual women, and 15 each of homosexual and heterosexual men) and the statistical methods, and concluded: "Data presented by Rahman *et al.* do not confidently support their finding that homosexual women exhibit a male-type startled-blink reflex."[54]

Harrison further stated that "no significant differences were detected."

As far as the blink reflex being utterly innate or somewhat trainable, he responded to an interviewer, "Now, that's an open question."[55] Dr. Harrison also said he would have liked to have seen the complete data on the series of tests to see whether the subjects' responses would change with repetition. This would indicate whether the PPI is entirely innate.

In his conclusion, he said: "This comment should not be construed as falsifying the hypothesis that homosexual and heterosexual women display different prepulse startle-inhibition reflexes. That conjecture may turn out to be so, but the present data do not confidently support it."

---

[53] Ibid., p. 1098.

[54] Halstead Harrison, "A Technical Comment on the paper, 'Sexual Orientation-Related Differences in Prepulse Inhibition of the Human Startle Response,'" University of Washington Web site, 15 December 2003, http://www.atmos.washington.edu/~harrison/reports/rahman.pdf.

[55] Telephone interview with Patrick Henry College senior and Culture & Family Institute intern Jeremy Sewall, 8 March 2004.

Neuroendocrine Hypotheses

In 1999, Dr. Qazi Rahman compiled a brief review of several studies purporting to show a link between neuroanatomy and sexual orientation.[56]

He wrote: "The emerging neuroanatomical account suggests that, in some key neural substrates, homosexual men show a trend toward female-typical neuroanatomy as compared to heterosexual men."[57]

Rahman also said, "Lesbians excel at some tasks which favor heterosexual males."

As in the eye-blinking study, Rahman struck a cautionary note: "But is neuroendocrine differentiation a cause or a consequence of behavior? . . . In addition, the differential development posited may not be causal but correlational."

Rahman noted that, "Differential reinforcements from inputs in the psychosocial milieu to these sex-atypical behaviors makes the 'pre-homosexual child' view the same sex as 'exotic' (i.e., different from one's self), which later in puberty becomes the object of eroticization."[58]

As some developmental psychologists have observed, some children may be less inclined to exhibit classic gender role differences, and this may set them up for the type of reactions from peers (or even parents), such as rejection or teasing, that make them vulnerable to developing same-sex attraction.[59]

One glaring problem with Rahman's article is that he uncritically cites many of the studies that were thoroughly debunked by researchers such as Columbia's Byne and Parsons. These include studies by LeVay, Hamer, Allen, Gorski, Bailey and others.

[56] Qazi Rahman, "Comments on the Neuroanatomy of Human Sexual Orientation and Proposed Neuroendocrine Hypotheses," *Journal of Contemporary Neurology*, The MIT Press, Vol. 1999, No. 2A.

[57] Ibid., p. 2.

[58] Ibid., p. 3.

[59] Numerous references to this phenomenon are reported throughout Joseph Nicolosi, Ph.D., *Reparative Therapy of Male Homosexuality* (Northvale, New Jersey: Jason Aronson, Inc., 1991).

Rahman wraps up his piece this way:

To conclude, it is important to illustrate that neurobiological differences between homosexuals and heterosexuals are by no means decisive. Nonetheless, the several independent findings of neuroanatomical differences in sex-atypical directions are not easily refutable. *[Editor's note: Yes, they are. Byne and Parsons, among others, saw to that.]* Unfortunately, evidence currently available is limited and largely correlational in nature. Owing to this, it is not possible for alternative developmental processes associated with sexual orientation to be excluded.[60]

Conclusion

Determining whether something has a biological cause is difficult, and locating a specifically genetic link is even more so. The handful of studies that purportedly add up to incontestable "proof" that homosexuals are "born that way" are inconclusive at best and, as Dr. Rahman notes, "largely correlational in nature." In some cases, such as the twins studies, the evidence strongly indicates that early environment is more likely the dominant factor to have produced homosexual desires.

As Dr. Satinover emphasizes, correlation does not mean something is causative. Basketball players are tall, so height correlates with playing basketball, he notes. But there is no "basketball-playing gene." Efforts to turn some interesting correlations into causal factors have not been successful and yet have been misused to advance a political agenda.

Perhaps the best way to describe the situation is this, as paraphrased from Dr. Satinover: Some people may be predisposed because of genetic, prenatal hormonal influences or other physical or brain differences to have personalities that make them vulnerable to the environmental factors that can

---

[60] Rahman, op. cit., p. 3.

elicit homosexual desires. So is homosexuality biological? Not in the way that popular media and homosexual activists have presented it.

Extremely shy and artistic young boys, for instance, who are not affirmed in their masculinity by a caring father, might be at risk for homosexuality. It's not because of a homosexual "gene," but because of an interrupted process of achieving secure gender identity. This can make some boys who crave male affirmation an easy mark for seduction into homosexuality. A similar pattern can be seen in girls who don't fit classic gender profiles, need feminine affirmation, and are targeted by lesbians who play upon the girls' emotional needs.

Such children's vulnerability is all the more reason to protect them from early exposure to homosexual influences. The Boy Scouts of America, for instance, is right to screen out as troop leaders those men who desire other males sexually. The Scouts do so not out of bigotry, or a belief that all homosexual men molest boys. They do so out of genuine concern for the health and well-being of the boys in their charge, including those who might be sexually vulnerable.

Americans for too long have been pummeled with the idea that people are "born gay." The people who most need to hear the truth are those who mistakenly believe they have no chance themselves for change. It is both more compassionate and truthful to give them hope than to serve them up politically motivated, unproven creations like the "gay gene."

> *"'I believe homosexual acts between two individuals are immoral and that we should not condone immoral acts.'"*

General Sparks Controversy by Denouncing Homosexual Acts

Catholic Insight

In the following viewpoint Catholic Insight, *reports on comments in 2007 by US Marine General Peter Pace, then chairman of the US Joint Chiefs of Staff, about homosexual acts as immoral, as well as comments by others in response. Opponents viewed the remarks as insensitive, intolerant, and disrespectful. Defenders viewed the remarks as expressing the view of a majority of Americans and supported by the Bible, the Koran, and natural law.* Catholic Insight *is a Catholic magazine that "endeavours to foster the culture of life by reporting truthfully, critically, contextually, and comparatively with a view to history and guided by a cultural vision inspired by Catholic doctrine and the classical liberal arts."*

As you read, consider the following questions:

1. What was the response of Speaker of the House, Nancy Pelosi, to Pace's comments, according to the author?

2. What was the response of author and attorney David Limbaugh to Pace's opponents, according to the viewpoint?

3. What correction does the author/editor offer in response to the Servicemembers Legal Defence Network statement about 65,000 lesbian and gay troops in the U.S. Armed Forces?

Washington, DC—Marine General Peter Pace, the chairman of the U.S. Joint Chiefs of Staff, sparked a controversy when he told the editorial board of the *Chicago Tribune* newspaper that, "I believe homosexual acts between two individuals are immoral and that we should not condone immoral acts. I do not believe the United States is well served by a policy that says it is okay to be immoral in any way." General Pace is a Catholic.

In response, the *Washington Post* chastised Pace for "his public expressions of intolerance on the men and women he commands." Speaker of the House, Nancy Pelosi, said: "We don't need a moral judgement from the chairman of the Joint Chiefs." The Servicemembers Legal Defence Network said in a statement that Pace's comments were "outrageous, insensitive and disrespectful" of what it claimed were 65,000 lesbian and gay troops in the U.S. Armed Forces. Democratic presidential contenders Hillary Clinton and Barack Obama both made it clear afterwards that they did not see homosexuality as immoral.

However, Pace's defenders saw it differently. *WorldNetDaily* editor Joseph Farah observed that Pace simply uttered a conviction shared by the vast majority of Americans, and the backlash against him was "clearly an effort to purge from authority anyone who dares represent the most basic tenets of the Judeo-Christian moral code."

Author and attorney David Limbaugh contended that if Pace's "unpardonable sin" was that of being judgemental,

Homosexuality Is Not Part of God's Design

Even if there is a genetic predisposition toward homosexuality (and studies on this point are inconclusive), the behavior remains unnatural because homosexuality is still not part of the natural design of humanity. It does not make homosexual behavior acceptable; other behaviors are not rendered acceptable simply because there may be a genetic predisposition toward them.

For example, scientific studies suggest some people are born with a hereditary disposition to alcoholism, but no one would argue someone ought to fulfill these inborn urges by becoming an alcoholic. Alcoholism is not an acceptable "lifestyle" any more than homosexuality is.

Catholic Answers, "Homosexuality." www.catholic.com.

"aren't many of his accusers guilty of the very same thing? Are they not passing moral judgement on and demeaning him for passing moral judgement on homosexual behaviour?"

Judge Roy Moore noted Pace's opinions comport with a long U.S. military tradition. He added that while men like Pace seek to defend the country from without, "we are being destroyed from within by those who want no part of virtue or morality."

Commentator and former presidential candidate Pat Buchanan said that on Pace's side are the Bible and the Koran, 2,000 years of Christianity, orthodox Judaism, natural law and the moral beliefs of virtually every society up to the recent past.

"What this uproar tells us is that America is no longer a moral community," he concluded. "On the most fundamental issues ... we are at war ... And where there is no moral community, there will not long be one country" (*WorldNetDaily*, Mar. 14, 16, and 21, 2007; *The Wanderer*, Mar. 29, 2007).

Editor: The claim of "65,000 lesbian and gay troops" is typically based on the myth that ten per cent of the population is homosexual, a Falsehood launched in the 1940s and long since disproven. One percent would be closer to the mark.

Second, in Canada the *Globe & Mail* said the General "should apologize to those he slurred with his comments" (Editorial, "No, sir, General Pace," Mar. 19, 2007). The *Globe* accused the general of maligning homosexuals, when the general had clearly restricted himself to homosexual acts as immoral, not about homosexuals as such.

I "*Homosexual Christians do not need a church that forces them to live a lie.*"

Homosexuality Is Not a Sin

Chris Ayers

Chris Ayers is the pastor at the Wedgewood Baptist Church in Charlotte, North Carolina. In the following viewpoint, Ayers relates personal anecdotes about his formative experiences with homosexuals and homosexuality. According to Ayers, as a youth, he learned to look down on homosexuality, creating a wall that protected his sense of secure masculinity. However, as he grew older, Ayers states that getting to know gay people helped him recognize that they were seeking love and compassion like everyone else. After becoming a preacher, Ayers has continued to advocate that the Christian Church accept homosexuals. He claims that the condemnation of homosexuals comes from a strict and selective reading of the Bible, and he maintains that Jesus Christ's actions and words show a more tolerant and loving view of humanity. Therefore, Ayers insists that homosexuality cannot be a sin and that learning to embrace homosexuals and all people may be a test the church must go through to make itself stronger and more committed to God.

As you read, consider the following questions:

1. What does Ayers say was the single most important factor that changed his opinion of homosexuality?

2. According to the author, what do homosexual Christians need from the church?

3. How did Jesus Christ, in Ayers's words, wipe out large chunks of the Bible with his statements and acts?

Let me begin by confessing an evil, wicked, shameful sin of mine. When I was a young boy, I—this is difficult to admit, very hard to say so please bear with me—when I was a young boy—gosh this is difficult—I didn't think it would be this hard to admit, but when I was a young boy I pulled for—Duke. Yes, I pulled for the Blue Devils (please notice that I put the emphasis on the word Devils)—I pulled for the Blue Devils when Vic Bubas was the coach and the team captain was Bob Verga.

My feeble attempt at a little differentiation, my oddness, my weirdness, my deviant behavior, did not go over too well with my family of origin. While my father and mother and two older brothers watched the Carolina/Duke game on the big television upstairs in the living room, I was sent downstairs to the basement to watch the game on a small television all by my lonesome self. I'm not making this up.

It did not take me long to repent for my sin. I wanted to be loved and accepted and to fit in. I wanted to belong, so I quickly became an obnoxious Carolina fan.

These days I'm only slightly obnoxious, but I'm still obnoxious enough to tell you that if I had my way, which since this is a Baptist church I don't get to have my way, but if I did have my way, we would not welcome and affirm Dookies. We might welcome them, as in allow them to sit on the pew and put money in the plate, but we definitely wouldn't affirm them.

Being Welcoming and Affirming

I guess that's the tricky thing about being a welcoming and affirming church. It's a real stretch to welcome and affirm everybody, particularly people who don't welcome and affirm you. For the record, I'm not real tolerant of intolerant people. I'm trying to work on that. I'm trying to work on that and be patient with others who I would like to slap silly because not too long ago I would have needed to have been slapped silly myself for some of the same stuff.

Which leads me to today's sermon, a sermon titled "Homosexuality Is Not a Sin: The Christian Education of a Baptist Minister." Or put another way, what I have to offer you is a good old-fashioned Baptist testimony. I grew up in one of those conservative Southern Baptist churches and giving your testimony was a big thing. Well, I have a testimony about what God has done in my life. To be sure, it's not your typical Baptist testimony. But it is a testimony; a testimony which I believe could have only been made possible by God. If anyone had told me 20 years ago I would no longer view homosexuality as a sin and that some of my best friends would be homosexuals I would have told them they were crazy. As you will hear, my journey has been a long one. That's why I say it has been an education. And I say it is a Christian education, because what I have learned has been learned in the context of the church and has been made possible by Christians who just happen to be gay or lesbian or bisexual. And as I said, I believe without the help of God I would not have gotten this Christian education.

Early Encounters with Homosexuality

So here's my Baptist testimony, with a little prophetic twist thrown in at the end for good measure.

Well, let's start in the beginning. I am in the fifth grade and I'm starting to notice girls, actually one girl in particular. While I'm noticing this beautiful female I also notice that a male classmate of mine, unlike me, does not appear to be noticing females. How he could not be impressed with this female I have my eye on confuses me. My classmate is pretty much a loner. He keeps to himself. And sadly he is the object of more than a few verbal abuses delivered by his classmates. Schoolchildren can be cruel.

At this point, I have no clue there are homosexuals in the world. I just know some people are odd, different, odd and different in more than just their personality. They don't fit in with the majority. And because they don't fit in, they pay a high price.

In middle school my education continues. I learn about more than calculus and U.S. history. I learn my family suspects we have a relative who is gay. He is a cousin. A fairly attractive person. He's not Robert Redford, but he is handsome enough not to have any trouble finding a woman. We start suspecting he is a homo, a fag—those are the terms we used. My cousin who is much older than me is not married, is not dating—dating a woman that is, and come to think of it, has never gone out with one of the XX chromosomes. This is odd because my cousin has a good bit of money and drives a nice sports car. If you are fairly attractive, have a big wad of money in your pocket, drive a red MG and you don't have a woman, the way we figure it—something's up.

About the same time we suspect there's a homosexual in the Ayers clan, a male friend of mine is dating a girl on the school basketball team who reports to him that her coach, who is a female, is a lesbian. This is a new vocabulary word for me. Never in my wildest imagination did it cross my mind that a woman would not want a man. We conclude this basketball coach is a pervert. We accuse her of being a predator, trying to make young heterosexual females into lesbians. We believe the woman should be fired immediately. She is horrible! She is disgusting!

From that day forward, we suspect all female coaches are lesbians whose intention is not to teach girls how to play a sport, but to see them naked in the locker room.

The middle school/high school years were interesting years. I call them the testosterone years. Our male voices deepened. Hair grew in new spots on our bodies. A lot of attention was given particularly to facial hair. Should I shave or should I not shave—this month?

Becoming a man, a man's man. Proving our masculinity. To do that we had to demonstrate we were more of a man than someone else. And so—and so we found easy targets, the weakest links. What better group of people to pick on than homosexuals. We didn't knowingly pick on a homosexual. In those days, we weren't familiar with the phrase coming out of the closet. No one in our class had fessed up to being a homo. But we did pick on homosexuals in the sense that we regularly called other males homosexuals as a way of shaming them, saying they were inferior. And chances are some of the people we called homosexual were homosexual.

An Important Relationship

The first crack in my cemented perspective came my freshman year at that great university in Chapel Hill. Living across 115 Lewis Residence Hall, living right across from my room, was a guy named Tim. Nice guy, and a Lutheran to boot. He got me to go one time to his Lutheran church and I discovered those Lutherans drink the real stuff. And they didn't call it The Lord's Supper. They called it some weird name, the Eucharist. Anyway, Tim invites me to a dorm Bible study on the 3rd floor led by a guy named Rick. I go for about a month. And then I start suspecting. There's that word again, suspecting. I suspect Rick is a homosexual.

I stop going to the Bible study and I forget about going to the Baptist Student Union [BSU]. I had had reservations about the BSU before I met Rick. I went to a few of the BSU meetings and I found the people to be real close to Jesus. So close, in fact, I wasn't worried they wouldn't make it to heaven; I feared they were going to overshoot heaven. Well, Rick was a big BSUer and that he was a homosexual was the straw that broke the camel's back. No way was I going to the BSU and hang out with a homo.

Rick knew what was going on with me. And he told me, "One day you are going to change."

Just what I needed, a homosexual Christian preaching to me.

But Rick turned out to be right. I did change, slowly, inch by inch. I changed to a great extent because of Tim.

I noticed Tim was going up to the third floor all the time. And it wasn't just for Bible study. He and Rick seemed to be hitting it off. Tim, all of a sudden, had a hop in his walk, a smile on his face, and he had gotten a tad feisty. All us men on the first floor of Lewis Residence Hall started suspecting. Suspecting not that Tim was a homosexual, but that evil Rick was trying to turn him into a homosexual.

We remained friends with Tim for a while. Tim went with us Lewis men to church, mostly to the Methodist church because the general consensus was the girls were better looking there. And we went out to eat with Tim, mostly to Bullock's BBQ in Durham which was the only good thing in Durham. But soon we made up a cruel rhyme about Tim, specifically, a rhyme about his sexual orientation. We said this in front of Tim repeatedly. And though the relationship at that point continued, it was never the same.

It was never the same.

The following year, I moved to south campus and I lost touch with Tim, but Tim forever changed me. Tim taught me all the things I had believed about gays were myths. And even though I did not like him, so did Rick. Both Tim and Rick are good people. Not perverts. Not weirdoes. Not predators. Not sick people. They are not all the things I had believed about

Sexual Orientation Is Not a Matter of Immorality

It is plain and simple prejudice to portray homosexuals as immoral just because of the gender to whom we are attracted. Of course there are immoral homosexuals, just as there are immoral heterosexuals, but simple orientation carries no implication of morality or immorality.

Our sexuality is God-given. God made us the way we are. It follows naturally that He loves us exactly the way He made us.

Mary Pearson,
"The Sin of Sodom Was Not Homosexuality!,"
Christian Gays, April 13, 2004. http://christiangays.com.

homosexuals. Tim and Rick are human beings with a deep faith. They are Christians. They are people with lives marked by integrity. I cannot argue with their lives. Oh, they were not and are not perfect, none of us are, but I cannot argue with their lives.

Getting to Know Gays and Lesbians

Getting to know Christians who just happen to be homosexual is the single most important factor that changed my mind, that transformed me.

My experience has been like that of [liberal Christian clergyman] William Sloane Coffin who writes, "What did the most to help me battle [my homophobia], more than the accumulation and analysis of the evidence available, was to spend time with gay people. Familiarity bred only respect, never contempt."

I am reminded of two quotes that appeared in the *Charlotte Observer.* A conservative Christian commenting on homosexuals said he "loved the sinner, but hated the sin." To which a Roman Catholic priest replied, "How can you love someone you do not know?"

Let me tell you something that is beautiful. We have had people come to Wedgewood and say up front that they don't want to be homophobic, that they would never want to do or say anything to harm a homosexual, but there's just something about homosexuality that makes them uneasy, uncomfortable. They admit there's a hurdle they haven't been able to get over. They say that, they are honest about it, and then something happens. They get to know, underline that word, they get to know, really know some gay and lesbian Christians and I see them changing before my very eyes. They see what I have seen, that some of the best Christians we have at Wedgewood are our homosexual members. And to paraphrase Jesus, they say, "not even among the heterosexual Christians have I found such faith."

When Christians talk to me about their reservations about gays and lesbians I ask them, Have you gotten to know the homosexuals in your faith community? And I say, Have you realized the presence of homosexuals in your church is a miracle? I believe any time a homosexual walks through the doors of a church it is a miracle. Why, why would anyone who has been rejected so much open himself or herself up to more rejection? . . .

Selective Interpretations of the Bible

Sad stories. I've heard them. I've seen the tears of gays and lesbians. I've heard them sob. I've heard them weep. Someone, some Christians, some church, needs to tell the world about the tears and say as boldly as possible that homosexuality is not a sin. Saying homosexuals should be tolerated is not enough. Saying homosexuals are welcome in a church just like all sinners are welcome is not enough. Saying gay and lesbian clergy can be clergy as long as they are celibate is not enough. The church needs to say boldly that homosexuality is not a sin.

Some people believe homosexuals choose to be homosexual. No, what I have witnessed are homosexuals choosing to deny their sexual orientation, some even going so far as marrying a person of the opposite sex and having children.

Homosexual Christians do not need a church that forces them to live a lie. They need love, acceptance, and affirmation. They need a church that has learned homosexuality is not a sin. They need a faith community which is honest about biblical interpretation.

Yes, the Bible. But what about the Bible?, some will ask. What about those verses that indicate homosexuality is a sin? How can you say homosexuality is not a sin when the Bible clearly says it is?

For those of you interested in a fuller treatment than time permits this morning, I recommend the work of Walter Wink. Here's a quick summary of Wink. Wink admits there are three passages that condemn same-sex behavior, far less texts than many use to buttress their anti-homosexual position. Wink, however, goes on to point out that those who wish to condemn homosexuals on the basis of Bible verses are not as enthusiastic about the Bible's teaching in Leviticus 20:13 that demands that everyone who performs homosexual acts must suffer the death penalty. You see, Jerry Falwell, the big Bible believer, really does not believe all of the Bible like he says he does. Even Jerry says homosexuals are to be loved. And yet, Leviticus 20:13 says that homosexuals should be killed, something no one in their right mind would support today. So let's be honest about our biblical interpretation. We are all selective.

And that is what Wink hammers away at, our biblical selectivity. He delineates twenty Hebrew sexual mores, noting that in contemporary society we agree with only four of them and disagree with sixteen. In other words, we are picking and choosing and what we are choosing to focus on is homosexuality while we ignore the other stuff.

I admit I pick and choose. I'm just asking you and other so-called Bible believers to admit it also. If you haven't yet admitted you pick and choose, please allow me to take a stroll through the Bible with you.

Now picking and choosing is a tricky thing. We tend to pick and choose that which supports our worldview, that which supports our theology. So we need to be careful about this. For often what we need to read, what we need to live, is what we reject so quickly. On the other hand, sometimes we pick and choose because we do not worship a book, but a God revealed to us in Jesus Christ, and we have enough sense to know that everything in the Bible does not match up to what we know about Jesus.

An Important Lesson for Christians and the Church

But here's another point that must be made. Jesus, himself, did not believe all of the Bible of his day. Jesus did some picking and choosing as well.

Plastered throughout the Old Testament is the idea that if you are good, God is going to bless you real good, and that includes financial blessings. If you are bad, well, bad things are going to happen to you. But—but when you come to Jesus, he says the rain falls on who? The just. Well, they knew that. But Jesus goes on to say that the rain also falls on the unjust. With that one statement Jesus wiped out, wiped out a large chunk of the Bible. And in that same passage when Jesus said love your enemy, Jesus also wiped out a huge portion of the Old Testament. All that killing they thought was the will of God was not the will of God.

Or consider the time Jesus came across a man born blind. The Bible of Jesus' day taught that if bad things happen to you it could be because of your sin or the sins of your parents, but Jesus said the man was not born blind because of his sin or his parents' sin and with that statement Jesus wiped out, wiped out a large chunk of the Bible.

And let's not forget Peter. Ever since Peter was a little boy he had been taught the book of Leviticus, taught what was clean and unclean. And then one day as an adult, he had a vision, a vision in which he was instructed the Bible he had read was wrong about what was unclean. Well, Peter was dumbfounded. He said, "No way Jose. The Bible wrong?" So the hard-to-accept vision came to him a second and a third time to get through his thick skull, his cemented perspective. Yes, Leviticus is wrong, Peter. What God has made clean, you must not, you must not call unclean.

My experience has been like that of Peter. I used to think homosexuality was wrong because the Bible said it was wrong. But I had a vision. Yes, I had a vision, a vision that came to me repeatedly. Because of some wonderful Christians who just happen to be gay and lesbian, I learned homosexuality is not a sin.

I told you I was going to throw in a little prophetic twist at the end. Here it is. Wouldn't it be ironic if gays and lesbians and bisexual and transgendered individuals turn out to be the salvation of the modern church? I believe, as [Bible scholar] Clarence Jordan put it, that the modern church has gone a-whoring. What if, what if homosexual Christians and others end up being the ones who rescue the modern church from its impotence, its infidelity, its arrogance, its dishonesty, its irrelevance, its neglect of the marginalized, its addiction to clergy, its obsession with power and bad money and property, its adoption of the business model, its focus on the trivial? What if, what if homosexual Christians turn out to be the ones who get the church to talk less about the faith and to spend more time actually doing something Jesus did? What if gays and lesbians teach the church how to love and accept and affirm?

This much I know. It was not very much fun being ostracized, watching the Duke/Carolina game downstairs on a small television all by myself. I suffered only a little, only for a short period. I cannot imagine the pain and suffering homosexuals experience. What I can imagine, though, is God using the pain and suffering of gay and lesbian and bisexual Christians to help the church once again be church.

Periodical and Internet Sources Bibliography

The following articles have been selected to supplement the diverse views presented in this chapter.

Michael Abrams   "The Real Story on Gay Genes," *Discover*, June 2007.

Nathan W. Bailey   "Different Flings for Different Wings," *Chronicle of Higher Education*, August 8, 2008.

Patrick J. Buchanan   "Blacklisted, but Not Beaten," *American Conservative*, March 2012.

Bryan Cones   "A Good Fit? Church Teaching on Homosexuality and Human Dignity," *US Catholic*, January 2012.

Emmanuele A. Jannini,   "Male Homosexuality: Nature or Culture?,"
Ray Blanchard, Andrea   *Journal of Sexual Medicine*, October 2010.
Camperio-Ciani, and
John Bancroft

William J. Jenkins   "Can Anyone Tell Me Why I'm Gay? What Research Suggests Regarding the Origins of Sexual Orientation," *North American Journal of Psychology*, June 2010.

Stanton L. Jones   "Same-Sex Science," *First Things*, February 2012.

Robert Kunzig   "Finding the Switch," *Psychology Today*, May/June 2008.

Jay Michaelson   "Dispelling the Myth of God Versus Gay," *USA Today Magazine*, November 2011.

Eric Reitan   "Gay Suicide and the Ethic of Love: A Progressive Christian Response," *Religion Dispatches*, October 12, 2010.

OPPOSING
VIEWPOINTS®
SERIES

CHAPTER 2

Should Same-Sex Marriage Be Legal?

Chapter Preface

In 1993 Hawaii nearly became the first state in the union to legally permit same-sex marriages. After three homosexual couples brought suit on the grounds that a state statute barring same-sex marriage violated their right to equal protection, the Supreme Court of Hawaii ruled that the state had to prove a compelling reason why the ban was permissible under Hawaii's constitution, which made no mention of the sexual orientation of those who could be legally wed. Because the court did not conclude that the ban was unconstitutional, the state legislature quickly amended the statute in question to specify marriage as a ceremony between a man and a woman, thus avoiding further litigation opportunities. The Hawaiian court case prompted opponents of same-sex marriage to organize nationwide to ensure similar statutes were in place in other states, fearing that if any state sought to condone same-sex marriage, then the other state governments—even the federal government—might be forced to recognize the legitimacy of the partnership under the full faith and credit clause of the Constitution, a portion of Article IV that maintains that all states must accept the validity of public acts and judicial proceedings that occur in any one state.

In 1996, after successful lobbying efforts, same-sex marriage opponents convinced their legislators in Washington to draft and pass the Defense of Marriage Act (DOMA), a bill that stipulates that the full faith and credit clause cannot be applied to same-sex marriage and that the federal government does not consider same-sex marriage as a valid compact for obtaining Social Security benefits for surviving spouses, receiving insurance benefits for government employees, or filing joint tax returns. Defending the appropriateness of DOMA's passage, Senator Trent Lott stated from the chamber floor, "To force upon our communities the legal recognition of same-sex marriage would be social engineering beyond anything in the American experience." Critics, however, were shocked by such rhetoric. Writing in the September/October issue of *Ms.*, executive editor Barbara Findlen argued, "Politicians and far-right activists have used this issue to feed into people's insecurities about the stability of traditional social institutions, and they have used it as a means to voice their own bigotry and fear. DOMA and the state bans on same-sex marriage have become a politically acceptable way to codify the second-class status of lesbians and gay men."

Though DOMA bars the portability of same-sex marriage across state borders, the states themselves have become the new battleground for sanctioning or banning these ceremonies. In 2004 Massachusetts became the first state to legalize same-sex marriage after the state supreme court ruled that it was unconstitutional to reserve marriage only for heterosexual couples. Recalling the Hawaii controversy a decade earlier, some states reacted to the Massachusetts ruling by writing into their constitutions the definition of marriage as a compact between a man and a woman. As of 2012, thirty-eight states have constitutional amendments or laws that limit marriage of same-sex individuals. Only nine states and the District of Columbia have authorized same-sex marriages as of 2012, with Maine, Maryland, and Washington being the most recent to recognize such unions.

The legalization of same-sex marriage in several states may be a sign that the nation is becoming more tolerant of these partnerships. Indeed, an NBC News/*Wall Street Journal* poll conducted in March 2012 revealed that national support for same-sex marriage has risen to 49 percent, while opposition has declined to 40 percent from a high of 62 percent in 2004. However, as the viewpoints in the following chapter attest, the debate is still hotly contested in moral and legal arenas across America.

> *"Same-sex couples are only asking for what is deserved, the extensions of these marriage rights that are open to our heterosexual peers."*

Same-Sex Marriage Supports the Civil Institution of Marriage

Jason Frye

In the following viewpoint, Jason Frye claims that marriage has always been predominantly a civil institution managed by the state. To him, it is a way for all couples to receive public recognition for their loving commitment and to garner the social privileges that the state accords such couples. To deny marriage to same-sex couples, Frye argues, is a means of depriving certain citizens of their rights and to sanction discrimination. As a humanist, Frye believes the religious motivations for banning same-sex marriage are no longer relevant in a society that has largely divorced civil policy from church edicts. Thus, he insists it is time to accept that marriage applies to all committed partners who enter willingly into that institution. Jason Frye is president of the Humanist Association of San Diego and the coordinator of the American Humanist Association's LGBT Humanist Council.

As you read, consider the following questions:

1. How does Frye use the *Loving v. Virginia* ruling to further his argument about accepting same-sex marriage?

2. Why does Frye maintain that "epistemologically theistic" arguments against same-sex marriage, however rational, are still problematic?

3. Why does Frye think it is important to use the word "marriage" to describe the state-supported commitment between same-sex couples?

On July 24 [2011] New York became the sixth state to offer officially recognized marriage licenses to same-sex couples; but it didn't recognize same-sex marriage. Why? Because there is no such thing. Though we hear these sexual orientation–oriented matrimonial distinctions ad nauseam, common usage does not confer definition. What saying "gay" or "same-sex" marriage does confer is that the social worth of gay and lesbian individuals is subordinate and inferior to their heterosexual counterparts.

Call It Marriage

As humanists, such degradations are not in the complement of our intentional vocabulary. As humanists, we should stop saying "gay marriage" and "same-sex marriage" and call it what it really is: marriage.

I'm a humanist celebrant who has had the honor of performing marriage ceremonies for both same- and opposite-sex couples, and I can tell you that the only essential difference between these unions is the gender combination of the dolls on the cake—that and the harassment and disproportionate difficulties experienced by the lesbian and gay couples from those creating and capitalizing on this issue to suit their own agendas.

So what is marriage? I would define marriage (ideally) as a long-held, established civil institution based upon cultural expectations of long-term (often lifelong) committed monogamy and mutual respect between two non-related adults participating in a mutually consensual, intimate relationship. Such a marriage is conjoined by a civilly recognized contract that generally confers civil and social privileges in the form of tax benefits, Social Security survivor benefits, and so forth. These are the essential elements of the marital relationship. Beyond philosophical abstracts, marriage is a cherished, challenging, and rewarding commitment between two individuals who love each other and who have their relationship recognized by the state for certain privileges and protections. The marriage arrangement is a platform for these two individuals to nurture each other, pursue developing their family, and ideally, to help each other develop into better human beings. Nowhere in that structure is the sex or gender of the participants relevant. What is relevant is the love, mutual respect, care, and commitment between the participants.

Marriage Is a Civil Institution

In the United States, marriage is universally a civil institution, as evidenced by the paperwork those getting married must all submit to the same place: not the church, but the state. It took us 180 years to dispel legally sanctioned anti-miscegenation with the *Loving v. Virginia* decision in 1967, overturning Virginia's Racial Integrity Law (1924), where the biblical reasoning went that God's intended "natural" racial segregation was being disrupted, which therefore necessitated harassment of interracial couples and the prohibition of them legally marrying. It then took another thirty-six years to nullify sodomy laws. In that 2003 case (*Lawrence v. Texas*), it was noted that these specifically antigay sodomy laws were recent, and that all previous sodomy laws were aimed at all forms of non-procreative forms of sexual encounter. Still, Justice An-

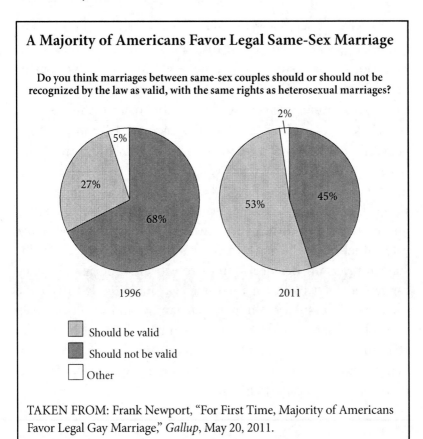

A Majority of Americans Favor Legal Same-Sex Marriage

Do you think marriages between same-sex couples should or should not be recognized by the law as valid, with the same rights as heterosexual marriages?

2%

5%

27%

68%

53%

45%

1996

2011

■ Should be valid

■ Should not be valid

□ Other

TAKEN FROM: Frank Newport, "For First Time, Majority of Americans Favor Legal Gay Marriage," *Gallup*, May 20, 2011.

thony Kennedy mentioned that the *Lawrence* court was not considering the right of homosexual individuals to marry each other. Even so, it is a progression, one that is becoming more rapid each day, leading us closer to a time when we'll look back and see this whole mess for the embarrassment that it is.

A Matter of Rights

We know that homosexuality is neither a disease nor a disorder. We also know that there is no valid secular reason to discriminate against gay and lesbian individuals in the areas of family, marriage, employment, and all other forms of political or social equality. Diminished social worth caused by popular disparaging has far-reaching consequences, including bullying, suicide, employment discrimination, and exclusion from deserved rights and benefits. Same-sex couples demanding deserved state recognition of their spousal relationships aren't seeking so-called same-sex tax breaks, same-sex hospital visitation, same-sex adoption of their spouse's children, or (in some cases) same-sex spousal immigration rights. Same-sex couples are only asking for what is deserved, the extensions of these marriage rights that are open to our heterosexual peers.

We can talk about the nature of reality. We can examine this issue with a critical eye and come to these conclusions of reason, but the problem remains that the perceived inferiority of homosexual and bisexual individuals tends to be a position of the epistemologically theistic. And in some ways, their position is more about misogyny than sexuality. After all, there are only a handful of biblical passages that can be construed as condemning homosexual behavior, but scores demonstrating the diminished worth of women. This being so, homophobia and heterocentrism are not ubiquitous interests for all religious or faith-based organizations. The arguments against a same-sex couple's right to receive equal marriage all too often come from a Bible draped in a plastic, one-sided American flag. They entail such perennial gems as "Adam and Eve, not Adam and Steve," and "Love the sinner, hate the sin."

The God Argument Is No Longer Current

In terms of intellectual currency, this God in absentia is no longer paying the bills. We no longer need a god for health and welfare, social order, or the maintenance of the laws of physics (and frankly, we never did). As with the God concept, statistically significant evidence for the efficacy of intercessory prayer is severely lacking (no God, no agency, no reason to continue paying attention). We've moved on, no matter how interesting it may be to wax philosophical about God's attributes.

And so, fundamentally, the religious arguments against recognizing marriage between same-sex couples are not just bad arguments, they're not our arguments, and they aren't even worth our time.

So stop saying it. Just stop saying "same-sex marriage." Doing so brings up the religious connotations of an arbitrary and fictional hierarchy of gender and sexuality. The religious say that things are "sinful" and as humanists we don't concur—so why should we with this? Accepting marriage as a civil institution, it doesn't make sense to laden ourselves with these unworkable constructs. Also, as a gay man, I find the implication of inferiority by distinction offensive. Simply calling it what it is—marriage—brings us to a point of honesty and openness, and sets a point of departure for discussion. Language has power, and without thinking, our use of these specific terms can cause pain and separation between us and the very people we support. Freethinkers are always at the forefront of pursuits to elevate all of humanity, to achieve equality, and to work for the greater good (which includes happiness). As humanists we must be compelled to actively participate in these endeavors. And while we don't always have time to write a letter, or a dollar or two to chip in, we do have the ability to do the little things that really matter, and this is one of them. So, once and for all, stop saying "same-sex marriage" and call it what it really is: marriage. For all.

"There is not a same-sex equivalent to bride and groom. To insist that there are such equivalencies, and to act on this error, not only represents marriage as something it is not but also envisions salvation as something it is not."

Same-Sex Marriage Violates the Sacrament of Marriage

Vigen Guroian

Vigen Guroian is a professor of religious studies at the University of Virginia in Charlottesville and the author of The Melody of Faith: Theology in an Orthodox Key *and other works. In the following viewpoint, Guroian argues that a same-sex union cannot be tolerated as part of the holy sacrament of marriage. As he explains, Christian marriage is not a civil partnership; it is a manifestation of God's will to join man and woman as one flesh bonded to Christ. Marriage is not a symbolic union, according to Guroian, but a religious practice that exemplifies God's prophecy and "fulfills the goal and purpose of Creation." For these reasons, Guroian insists that it excludes same-sex partners. To keep the religious nature of marriage intact, Guroian suggests that the*

Vigen Guroian, "Let No Man Join Together," *Touchstone: A Journal of Mere Christianity*, vol. 24, no. 1, January/February 2011, pp. 28–32. Copyright © 2011 by Touchstone: A Journal of Mere Christianity. All rights reserved. Reproduced by permission.

government perform civil ceremonies while allowing churches to enact the marriage sacrament subsequently on those who conform to the model put forth by God.

As you read, consider the following questions:

1. In what part of courtship does Guroian claim that "consent" between partners belongs, according to Orthodox teachings?

2. What civil problems does the author foresee if marriage is no longer defined as a sacrament between man and woman?

3. How does Guroian think the Orthodox Church should respond to the civil tolerance of same-sex marriage?

In recent years, homosexual persons and their supporters in North America have argued that marriage should be redefined to include the union of two persons of the same sex. Increasingly, this argument has been cast as a civil liberties issue: homosexual persons seek constitutional rights and liberties that have long been denied to them, key among these being marriage.

Same-sex marriage, however, is not just a legal matter. It is also a religious issue. For millennia, Western civilization has strictly understood marriage to be the union between a man and a woman. This definition, grounded in biblical beliefs about the nature of God and humanity, was reflected in common morality and civil law. Only recently has this understanding been questioned.

At present, the debate is principally over marriage between homosexual persons, but it is not likely to remain so. For if our society extends the boundaries of marriage's meaning beyond the union of a man and a woman, there will remain no compelling reason under the law to deny "marital" status to heterosexual same-sex partners who seek the benefits that come with it, or, for that matter, to persons in polygamous relationships. This will explode the historical meaning of marriage that has [existed] in our culture for millennia.

Under these circumstances, the gay and same-sex marriage issue obliges Orthodox Christians to be very clear about their church's theology of marriage, and why a partnership—and *partnership* is the appropriate term, not *union* or *marriage*—of any sort between persons of the same sex is not in character nuptial.

The Legacy of Rome

In pagan Rome during the first centuries of the Christian era, marriage was one of several acceptable forms of cohabitation and family life, and was available as a legal status only to free citizens. If two such persons, man and woman, lived together by consent in a regularized fashion and assumed the roles and responsibilities of husband and wife, then they were considered married under the law.

Roman law stipulated that marriage in its essence was not about intercourse but the free consent of the individuals entering into it. Marriage would exist, therefore, where there was the intention to form a household and did not require legal formalization, though that was available and qualified a couple for the special privileges accorded marriage. These included passing down the family name to children and inheritance of the father's estate by the legitimate offspring of the marriage.

To this day, Western Christian understandings of marriage strongly reflect the Roman principle of consent. This consensual view of marriage became dominant in Latin and Western Christianity as the church ingested Roman law. To one degree or another, in Roman Catholic and Protestant traditions alike, consent was "baptized" as a central element of marriage. The Roman Catholic Church eventually defined marriage as a sacrament, but the principle of consent has been at least as important in its theology of marriage. The principle of consent lies behind the Roman Catholic Church's belief that the bride and groom administer their marriage to one another and is reflected in its denial of divorce. . . .

In the Orthodox tradition, however, consent was not "baptized" as the validation or essence of a marriage. The clerical officer (bishop or priest), representing the church, marries the bride and groom, and the couple is by this act bonded as husband and wife to Christ and the church. The conjugal love union is understood to be at the heart of marriage. Marriage is a sacrament of love. This love union is founded and grounded in God's will, in his creative act of making humankind male and female, so that, through their love for one another and sexual union, a man and a woman may become "one flesh."[*]

Marriage Is Not Founded on Consent

Nevertheless, many North Americans who identify themselves as Christians, including Orthodox, quite simply assume that the couple's consent seals the marriage; that in a practical sense the will of the couple brings the marriage into existence and the withdrawal of this will is sufficient to terminate it. Present secular marriage and divorce law reflect this. My point is simply that the principle of free consent remains fixed as a cultural norm even as a contemporary people forget the sacred meaning and sacramental significance of marriage.

This principle of consent, and the logic supporting it, is what today enables the advocates of gay marriage to make great headway in the legislature and the courts—and within the churches, especially Protestant churches that lack a sacramental understanding of marriage. It should surprise no one that, as the belief diminishes in these churches that homosexual acts are sinful, unnatural, or psychopathically abnormal, the argument for gay marriage will gain plausibility and persuasiveness among their adherents.

[*] Consent more properly belongs to Orthodox betrothal practices.

There prevails among many religious as well as secular people the belief that when two homosexual persons desire and freely consent to share their lives with one another as a domestic couple, the state should grant this partnership legal status as a marriage. And many, also, are coming to believe that the churches should solemnize these civilly contracted same-sex unions as Christian marriages.

Since this logic of consent is deeply embedded in our culture and in modern jurisprudence, it is easy to imagine that the sorts of changes in marriage law and tax codes that the gay lobby is seeking may eventually be extended to other same-sex households that are not homosexual. How could the state possibly discriminate—or even ask the questions needed to discriminate—between homosexual and heterosexual couples of the same sex that come to get licensed? If marriage is no longer defined as strictly between a man and a woman, why shouldn't widows or widowers, brothers or sisters, and the like, who live together for mutual assistance and economic reasons, be granted licenses for domestic partnerships that entitle them to the legal benefits and protections now accorded to married couples?

It may well be that the law ought to grant some of the privileges of marriage to some of these household arrangements, just so long as the law remains clear that marriage is between a man and a woman. The logic of the law and the modern egalitarian ethos, under the pressure of gay marriage advocacy, seem, however, to be pressing in a direction that will stretch the definition of marriage far beyond all historically recognizable bounds. This may sit well with a secular government, but such a redefinition of marriage cannot be acceptable to the church.

A Two-Tiered Arrangement

This rising challenge to the traditional understanding of marriage is emblematic of the crossroads at which our society is poised. And it places Orthodox and other Christians in an agonizing countercultural position whether they like it or not. This requires careful navigation, at least as careful and considered, and needing as much attention and wisdom, as the period that began with the emperors Theodosius I and Theodosius II of the fourth and fifth centuries and continued through Justinian in the sixth century.

For this was the period in which Christianity became the official religion of the Empire and the great codes were promulgated that truly defined and shaped Christendom. This has been our legacy until today, when the heart and spirit of Christendom are, alas, being banished from North American soil and the last remnants of these codes, which privileged marriage, supported sanctions against abortion and suicide, and provided for public prayer and the observation of Christian holy days, are being cleansed from the land.

For reasons that in this [viewpoint] I can only sketch out, it is advisable that Orthodox churches in such states as Massachusetts, New Hampshire, and Connecticut cease to cooperate or collaborate with the government in marrying persons, as has been done in one form or another within Christendom since the fifth and sixth centuries. I have urged my own church, the Armenian Orthodox Church, to act in this manner.

Such action would bring about a de facto two-tiered arrangement in which Orthodox Christians would obtain a civil marriage to meet the legal requirement and qualify for married status before the state, and then come to the church to receive the sacrament or marital blessing. Even under present arrangements, two marriage certificates are issued in most states, one religious and the other civil. Henceforth, the church would no longer assume responsibility for consecration of the civil contract.

By so acting, the church would lodge its profound disagreement with the state's unilateral and theologically erroneous redefinition of marriage. And the difference between marriage within the Body of Christ and the new forms of "marriage" that society has invented would be made clear. . . .

Sacramental Union

The world is itself sacramental. In other words, it is epiphanic of God its Creator. The appointed sacraments of the church are not exceptional (super) realities; they are not magic. Rather, they are specifications of the symbolical ontology of Creation; and they witness to the fact that humankind is created in the image of God. Each of the sacraments names and employs particular "natural" elements, reveals their epiphanic character, and employs their inherent capacity to serve God's salvific purpose.

Bread and wine are natural symbols of flesh and blood. Christ reveals them as symbols of his body and blood, in and through which he is verily present; and by consuming these translated elements, we enter into the most intimate communion with him as one ecclesial body.

Male and female are the exclusive elements and symbols of transformation in the sacrament of marriage. Marriage brings male and female together as God originally intended them: as spouses and companions to one another, husband and wife, one Christic and ecclesial being (Eph. 5:30–32). Through the sacrament, God heals our divided humanity at the primary source of its division, the alienation of male and female; he renders it whole once again; he restores male and female natures to their original unity and integrity.

This sacramental union of bride and groom is no mere cipher or allegory of human relationality, as represented by some proponents of gay marriage. Bride and groom are not nominal titles that may be bestowed upon any two persons, irrespective of their sex or gender, who enter into a "loving relationship." There is nothing incidental, accidental, or volitional about heterosexual humanity, or the fact that the male

The Danger of Banning Moral Discourse from the Same-Sex Marriage Debate

A danger may await us in the event that traditional views of sexual morality are overthrown and same-sex marriage is established. We see a sign of it in the driving of Catholic Charities out of adoption services in Massachusetts. The freedom to participate fully in civic life, to offer oneself to others in civil society, conscientiously on one's own terms as a religious person professing one's beliefs, may be jeopardized by this new dispensation. . . .

As we have seen in rulings like that of Judge [Vaughn] Walker [who struck down a proposition that banned same-sex marriage] in California [in 2010]—or the Iowa Supreme Court [that legalized same-sex marriage] in 2009—the argument made against the defenders of conjugal marriage is that they want to enact a religious agenda as public policy. As religious people, we are assured, they're entitled to think "privately" whatever they please about such matters—but not to enact their view as law because, as a religious view, it is somehow by definition "irrational." Even the possibility that their view of morality could be rational, and be rationally accessible to people not sharing their religion, is dismissed out of hand. The moral is collapsed into the religious; the religious is declared to be the irrational; and the irrational is declared to have no place in public policy.

Matthew J. Franck,
"Religion, Reason, and Same-Sex Marriage,"
First Things, *May 2011.*

is groom and the female is bride, or that the marital union of a man and a woman is an icon of the eschatological union of Christ and the church.

Christ is the groom and the church is his bride of the New Creation. The referent of groom is the eternal first man, Adam, and the referent of bride is the eternal first woman, Eve. The nuptial Adam-Eve humanity of the Book of Genesis, the first book of the Bible, is the analogue of the heavenly nuptials of the marriage of the lamb in the Book of Revelation (19:7), the last book of the Bible. The creation of nuptial humanity is an epiphany of the eternal humanity of God precedent to its complete revelation in the Incarnation. The creation of nuptial humanity is a prophecy of the church, which itself, through its nuptial union with Christ, fulfills the goal and purpose of Creation.

Human willing and choosing cannot change marriage's essence, or the symbolism that God has ordained for it. Thus, there simply is no such thing as same-sex marriage.* There is not a same-sex equivalent to bride and groom. To insist that there are such equivalencies, and to act on this error, not only represents marriage as something it is not but also envisions salvation as something it is not. . . .

Defending a Religious Practice

Sometimes, the children of God need to be wise as the serpent. They would be wise to contemplate the possibility that in the United States the day might arrive when the state, through legislative fiat or court decision, attempts to take marriage back from the church completely and place it exclusively under its own control. The free exercise clause of the Constitution would then be crucial to the defense of marriage. Churches would need to lean on it heavily to keep and defend holy matrimony.

---

* Whether or not individuals who seek a same-sex mariage are homosexual or heterosexual is not what is theologically decisive.

The best position from which to mount this defense is in the legitimate claim that Christian marriage is integral to Christian worship, is a sacrament and a Eucharistic feast.[*] Any attempt that the state might make to require churches to marry same-sex couples, therefore, would amount to an unconstitutional interference with religious practice, as the state would be unilaterally and unconstitutionally redefining a religious sacrament.

St. Theodore the Studite, in the ninth century, mentions two elements that belonged to Eucharistic marriage as early as the fourth century. He informs us that a crowning ceremony existed, followed by a brief prayer, a prayer that is virtually replicated in Orthodox rites of marriage:

> Thyself, O Master, send down Thy hand from Thy holy dwelling place and unite these Thy servant and Thy handmaid. And give to those whom thou unitest harmony of minds; crown them into one flesh; make their marriage honorable; keep their bed undefiled, deign to make their common life blameless.

This simple blessing encapsulates the entire meaning of Christian marriage. It is God who marries man and woman, and who is present at every Christian marriage. Christian marriage is a sacrament. It is a holy institution and divine call to discipleship. And through marriage, God opens up the gates of the kingdom of heaven to man and woman in their one-flesh union, as he made them to be in the beginning when he placed them in the garden of delight.

A Call to Reason

Now hear that portion of the Armenian rite of matrimony that immediately follows the hymn of betrothal, when the bride and groom face one another to receive the priestly bless-

---

[*] The early Christian apologists insisted upon the mystical connection between "marriage in the Lord" and the Eucharist.

ing. They stand facing each other as two complementary presences of a single humanity, once divided, that God now reunites. With his own hand, the priest joins the right hands of the bride and the groom. Then he states:

> God took the hand of Eve and gave it into the right hand of Adam. And Adam said: This is bone of my bones and flesh of my flesh. . . . Wherefore them that God has joined together, let no man separate. . . . See my dear children in Christ, according to the divine command and the ordinances of the holy fathers of the church, you have come to this holy church in order to be crowned and wedded in holy matrimony. May God keep you in mutual love, lead you to a ripe old age, and make you worthy of the incorruptible crown in heaven.

Can it be right for a priest of the Armenian Church to use the very same hand with which, as a minister of God, he joins bride and groom in holy matrimony, to sign a license of marriage for a state that has unilaterally redefined the meaning of marriage into something it is not? I, in conscience, have to say, "This cannot be so."

My aim in this [viewpoint] has been to set forth in a reasonably brief space an Orthodox response to the gay marriage and same-sex union debate. This response was intentionally theological, but its larger purpose is to lay the groundwork on which churches in America can defend marriage in the public sphere and protect it against the radically new notions of marriage that today are being constructed and enacted into law. This [viewpoint] is an invitation to Christians of all confessions to think about and reason through how they are going to respond to the grave challenge of same-sex marriage.

> "If it is a legitimate purpose for the respective states to define marriage, then it must be appropriate for the federal government to do so, at the least, to promote uniformity across its various territorial possessions and myriad government programs."

The Defense of Marriage Act Is an Essential Federal Law

Christopher M. Gacek

In the following viewpoint, Christopher M. Gacek asserts that the Defense of Marriage Act (DOMA) of 1996 is still a vital piece of national legislation. Gacek believes that marriage needs to be protected from the same eroding moral standards that have undermined family and marital commitment since the post–World War II era and the onset of the sexual revolution. Gacek maintains that same-sex marriage is the latest attempt to further subvert American institutions and the right of each state to protect those institutions. DOMA, in Gacek's opinion, preserves the traditional model of marriage as a heterosexual union and guarantees the right of the states to enforce that concept. A political

*scientist and author, Christopher M. Gacek serves as a senior fel-
low for regulatory affairs at the Family Research Council, an organization that promotes public policy centered on traditional
family values.*

As you read, consider the following questions:

1. As Gacek writes, which US president signed the Defense
   of Marriage Act into law?

2. As Gacek explains, what is the full faith and credit
   clause of the Constitution, and why is it important in
   the debate over marriage?

3. According to the author, proponents of same-sex marriage have avoided taking on DOMA's revision of the
   full faith and credit clause in favor of attacking what?

The federal Defense of Marriage Act, signed into law in
September 1996, is a vital element in preserving traditional marriage in America for two reasons. First, it protects
the law-making capacity of the various states in the field of
family law. It does this by making it possible for the states to
define marriage as the union of one man and one woman
without fear that the U.S. Constitution's full faith and credit
clause will be used by the courts to trump their marital policies. Thus, the Defense of Marriage Act allows each state to
formulate its own public policies, rather than be railroaded
into accepting the marriage norms of a few outlying socially
liberal states. Second, the act defines marriage traditionally for
purposes of federal law, thereby preventing novel and unjusti-
fied interpretations of federal statutes and regulations. This
aspect of the law has ensured much-needed uniformity across
federal law and programs.

In order to understand how and why the Defense of Marriage Act became law, it is necessary to look back at the history of judicial activism in the twentieth century, particularly

as it relates to the sexual revolution, the divorce revolution, and the homosexual rights revolution.

The Judiciary Overturns Traditional Laws and Mores

Over the past fifty years, the United States has witnessed a social revolution in which cultural and governmental elites have attempted to overturn—often successfully—age-old social-political institutions and mores. Quite often, the values under attack have dealt with familial and sexual relations. Though democratic change through legislative means has certainly been a part of the revolution, such changes in fundamental values could not always be accomplished democratically. Then, the courts have been more than willing to step in and force social transformation on the nation. It is not too much to say that the courts and the unelected bureaucracies of the administrative state—our new, fourth branch of government—now constitute powerful elements of an oligarchy unapologetically resistant to democratic influences.

After the Second World War, the judiciary actively took aim at the then current understanding of church-state relations and changed the relevant constitutional law—law that cannot be amended or overturned by legislatures. This process started with the U.S. Supreme Court's 1947 decision in *Everson v. Board of Education*. *Everson* was highly significant for two reasons. First, it held that actions of the states must satisfy the principles of the establishment clause of the First Amendment to the U.S. Constitution, whereas until that decision the establishment clause was deemed to apply only to the actions of the federal government. Second, *Everson* promulgated a forceful secular approach to First Amendment law, captured by its repetition of [Thomas] Jefferson's phrase describing "a wall of separation between church and state."

The line of cases following *Everson* invalidated many useful governmental policies and practices that were deemed by courts to have religious designs or effects. However, in recent years there has been a powerful intellectual counterattack to the historical and legal foundation of *Everson* and its progeny. Still in its early stages, this corrective effort has only begun to roll back the damage done by the courts in this area and probably awaits the advent of the next generation of lawmakers and jurists before its full impact will be felt.

Similarly, the secular elites of the legal profession and the political classes moved to revise the nation's laws and mores regarding marriage, the family, and sexuality. The sexual revolution, for example, was advanced by Supreme Court decisions involving contraceptives and the creation of a "right to privacy" (*Griswold v. Connecticut* (1965)). That right—for married couples to purchase and use contraceptives—was expanded to include unmarried persons in *Eisenstadt v. Baird* (1972). This progression led to the court's finding that the Constitution contains the right to abort an ongoing pregnancy and kill an embryo or fetus *in utero* (*Roe v. Wade* (1973); *Doe v. Bolton* (1973)).

The Implications of Changing Divorce Laws

The institution of marriage was not left undisturbed by the social-sexual tsunami that began to sweep over American institutions in the first half of the twentieth century. Many decades before Associate Justice Antonin Scalia's 2003 observation that the U.S. Supreme Court "ha[d] taken sides in the culture war," the court actively took steps making it easier for one marital partner to avoid the divorce laws of his or her state of marital domicile.

In these landmark cases, the foremost issues related to the recognition of out-of-state divorce decrees. Legal problems surrounding such factual circumstances existed for some time, but the Supreme Court began a dramatic revision of its interpretation of U.S. constitutional law starting in the 1940s. In a law review article on federalism, divorce law, and the Constitution, Professor Ann Laquer Estin of the University of Iowa College of Law notes:

> American divorce law was transformed by the Supreme Court in a series of decisions beginning with *Williams v. North Carolina* in 1942. These constitutional full faith and credit cases resolved a long-standing federalism problem by redefining the scope of state power over marital status. With these decisions, the court shifted from an analysis based on the competing interests of different states to an approach that highlighted the individual interests of the parties involved. This change fundamentally altered state power over the family by extending to individuals greater control of their marital status.

Professor Estin notes that "[e]ditorial comments after [the 1942 *Williams* decision] viewed the case as a triumph for the Nevada divorce mills." More significantly, the Supreme Court brought about an important change in divorce law that allowed individual decisions to trump the interests of families and of the family as an institution. The "divorce revolution" of the 1960s and 1970s was made possible by, and flowed from, the logic of these earlier decisions.

The Sexual Revolution Empowers Homosexuals

At the same time that American courts were upending long-standing legal relationships as described above, sexual behavior in the United States was undergoing a radical transformation. Not surprisingly, the "divorce revolution" occurred in parallel with the "sexual revolution." One aspect of the sexual revolution was the vigorous effort to have homosexual behavior accorded equal status with heterosexual behavior, despite three thousand years of Judeo-Christian orthodoxy—the foundation of Western moral law—arguing to the contrary. Not surprisingly, discussions of the formal recognition of same-sex relationships have existed for some time. According to Peter Sprigg of the Family Research Council, "[d]iscussions of homosexual 'marriage' among homosexuals themselves can be traced back at least fifty years." Public awareness of such intentions did not become known to mainstream America until the 1990s, however, when the real possibility arose that one state would legally recognize same-sex marriages.

The Defense of Marriage Act Defines Marriage in America

In May 1993 it appeared that Hawaii would become the first state to enact same-sex marriage after the state's highest court indicated that limiting marriage to one-man-one-woman couples was probably unconstitutional under Hawaiian law. A long process of litigation and state political upheaval followed.

Eventually, Hawaii retained its traditional definition of marriage in November 1998 after the state constitution was amended by referendum to read: "The legislature shall have the power to reserve marriage to opposite-sex couples." In December 1999, the Hawaii Supreme Court held that "[i]n light of the marriage amendment, [Hawaii's 1985 traditional marriage statute] must be given full force and effect." That ended Hawaii's marriage debate.

Nevertheless, the controversy had not been confined to Hawaii. Opinion leaders, legal scholars, and political leaders across the nation reacted to the 1993 court decision with the fear that Hawaiian same-sex marriages could be used by federal and state courts to overturn the marriage policies of the other forty-nine states. Thus, on September 21, 1996, three years before Hawaii settled its marriage debate, President William Jefferson "Bill" Clinton signed the Defense of Marriage Act ("DOMA") into law.

DOMA was intended to defend traditional marriage at the federal and state levels. Consequently, DOMA enabled states— even in the face of claims made pursuant to the full faith and

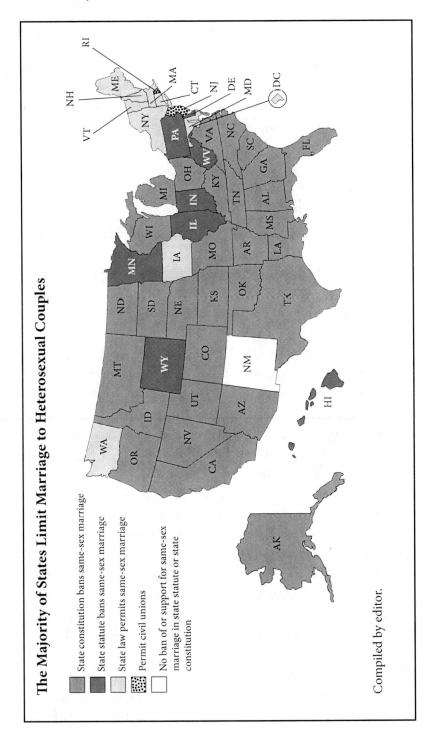

The Majority of States Limit Marriage to Heterosexual Couples

State constitution bans same-sex marriage

State statute bans same-sex marriage

State law permits same-sex marriage

Permit civil unions

No ban of or support for same-sex marriage in state statute or state constitution

Compiled by editor.

credit clause (discussed below)—to decline to recognize same-sex marriages from other states. Furthermore, DOMA defined marriage traditionally in federal law.

The Full Faith and Credit Clause

When the Constitutional Convention convened in Philadelphia in 1787, relations between the states were not ideal. In particular, there were problems with states declining to recognize the financial judgments rendered by the courts of other states. If debts could not be enforced across state lines, the United States would have significant problems with respect to promoting interstate commercial activity. To rectify this problem and to assist in unifying the country, the new Constitution contained a provision known as the "full faith and credit clause" (Article IV, Sec. 1), which states as follows:

> Full faith and credit shall be given in each State to the public Acts, Records, and judicial Proceedings of every other State. And the Congress may by general Laws prescribe the Manner in which such Acts, Records and Proceedings shall be proved, and the Effect thereof.

During the ratification debates, James Madison discussed this provision of the Constitution, noting that it constituted "an evident and valuable improvement on the clause relating to this subject" over its treatment in the Articles of Confederation. In addition to financial judgments, the full faith and credit clause has also been the basis for the interstate recognition of various decrees and judgments related to family law. As such, in 1996 it was regarded by Congress as the primary vehicle by which courts could compel states to recognize out-of-state same-sex marriages.

In 1790 Congress acted pursuant to the enhanced powers granted by the Constitution's full faith and credit clause by passing legislation putting the provision's intended purpose into effect. This law is often referred to as the "full faith and credit statute." Amended most recently in 1948, the statute provides, in part, that properly authenticated ". . . Acts, records and judicial proceedings or copies thereof ... shall have the same full faith and credit in every court within the United States and its Territories and Possessions as they have by law or usage in the courts of such State, Territory or Possession from which they are taken."

Allowing States to Define Marriage

DOMA affirms the power of each state to make its own decision as to whether it will accept or reject same-sex marriages created in other jurisdictions. This is accomplished by DOMA's second section, which amends the full faith and credit statute by adding this provision:

> No State, territory, or possession of the United States, or Indian tribe, shall be required to give effect to any public act, record, or judicial proceeding of any other State, territory, possession, or tribe respecting a relationship between persons of the same sex that is treated as a marriage under the laws of such other State, territory, possession, or tribe, or a right or claim arising from such relationship.

According to the House report on DOMA, Section 2 of the act was intended "to protect the right of the States to formulate their own public policy regarding the legal recognition of same-sex unions, free from any federal constitutional implications that might attend the recognition by one State of the right for homosexual couples to acquire marriage licenses." To that end, this section "provides that no State shall be required to accord full faith and credit to a marriage license issued by another State if it relates to a relationship between persons of the same sex." ...

Defining Marriage in Federal Law

DOMA contains another, equally important, provision. Section 3 of the statute defines marriage in federal law as follows (1 U.S.C. § 7):

In determining the meaning of any Act of Congress, or of any ruling, regulation, or interpretation of the various administrative bureaus and agencies of the United States, the word "marriage" means only a legal union between one man and one woman as husband and wife, and the word "spouse" refers only to a person of the opposite sex who is a husband or a wife.

The House report on DOMA summarizes this section of the statute as defining "the terms 'marriage' and 'spouse,' for purposes of federal law only, to reaffirm that they refer exclusively to relationships between persons of the opposite sex." The report noted that "[t]he word 'marriage' appears in more than 800 sections of federal statutes and regulations, and the word 'spouse' appears more than 3,100 times." Furthermore, it acknowledged that "[w]ith very limited exceptions, these terms are not defined in federal law." Therefore, a uniform federal definition of these terms was needed. . . .

Both sections of DOMA can easily be defended from anti-discrimination challenges. As [Stanford Law School professor Michael] McConnell [has] noted, Section 2 can withstand equal protection claims for the following reason:

> As held in the recent case of *Romer v. Evans*, 116 S. Ct. 1620, 1627 (1996), laws that disadvantage individuals on the basis of sexual orientation will be upheld so long as they bear "a rational relation to some legitimate end." The provision struck down in *Romer*, the court held, was not "directed to any identifiable legitimate purpose or discrete objective." *Id.* at 1629. By contrast, it is surely a legitimate legislative purpose to ensure that each state is able to make and enforce its own criteria for recognition of marriage.

Arguably, if it is a legitimate purpose for the respective states to define marriage, then it must be appropriate for the federal government to do so, at the least, to promote uniformity across its various territorial possessions and myriad government programs.

The Danger of Repealing DOMA

As of June 2010 twenty-nine states had adopted constitutional amendments restricting marriage to a relationship between one man and one woman, the first being Nebraska in 2000 and the most recent being California ("Prop 8"), Florida, and Arizona in 2008. Twelve additional states have statutes restricting marriage to one man and one woman. Thus, a total of forty-one states explicitly define marriage traditionally either through their state constitutions or by statutes. Some states also limit the scope of civil unions or domestic partnerships. Others have taken no action and rely on their laws that predate the current, post-Hawaii push for same-sex marriage recognition.

On the other side of the ledger, five states and the District of Columbia issue marriage licenses to same-sex couples. They are: Connecticut (2008), District of Columbia (2010), Iowa (2009), Massachusetts (2004), New Hampshire (2010), and Vermont (2009). [New York passed a law permitting same-sex marriage in June 2011. Washington State, Maine, and Maryland subsequently passed similar laws in 2012.] Given the number of states recognizing same-sex marriage, it is inevitable that a same-sex married couple will travel or move to another state and seek recognition of their same-sex marriage pursuant to the full faith and credit clause. If a court were to strike down or Congress were to repeal DOMA's full faith and credit clause provision, it would be much more difficult for a traditional-marriage state to hold the line in not recognizing another state's same-sex marriages. There would no longer be a statutory provision telling courts that the full faith and credit clause cannot be used to require one state to give effect to another state's judgments with respect to the recognition of same-sex marriages.

Interestingly, proponents of same-sex marriage seem wary of launching a frontal attack on DOMA's full faith and credit clause provision. Rather, they have chosen to attack the federal definition of marriage—as they have with state definitions of marriage. Most notably, the attorney general of the Commonwealth of Massachusetts, Martha Coakley, has challenged the constitutionality of DOMA's definition of marriage (1 U.S.C. § 7). Additionally, some members of Congress would like to repeal the federal definition of marriage.

As one Department of Justice brief noted, DOMA's traditional definition of marriage merely "continues the longstanding federal policy of affording federal benefits and privileges on the basis of a centuries-old form of marriage, without committing the federal government to devote scarce resources to newer versions of the institution that any State may choose to recognize." Furthermore, DOMA's traditional definition prevents federal bureaucrats from using rule makings (regulations) to develop alternative definitions of marriage for federal programs. Uniform federal law is efficient and just. DOMA has kept federal and state definitions of marriage aligned for the overwhelming majority of states that define marriage as being between one man and one woman. Finally, as made clear by Professor McConnell, DOMA does not violate the equal protection requirements of the Fourteenth Amendment to the U.S. Constitution.

Preserving States' Rights and Marriage

The Defense of Marriage Act preserves the right of the states to govern themselves with respect to family law and domestic relations. DOMA impedes judicial activism regarding marriage and provides needed uniformity in federal law. It is an essential part of preserving traditional marriage in America, and as then congressman [from California] Tom Campbell noted in 1996, it is "essential to preserving a union of states." Therefore, it is vital that the Defense of Marriage Act be maintained as it was enacted and signed into law in 1996. All efforts to nullify it judicially or repeal it legislatively must be resisted with all available resources.

> "The [Defense of Marriage Act], often
> called DOMA, denies federal recogni-
> tion of gay marriage and gives states
> the right to refuse to recognize same-
> sex marriages performed in other
> states."

Obama Administration Says Marriage Law Unfair

Devlin Barrett

*Devlin Barrett is a contributor to the Associated Press. In the
following viewpoint, Barrett contends that the President Barack
Obama administration believes the federal marriage law to be
discriminatory, and that it supports the repeal of the Defense of
Marriage Act (DOMA). Barrett maintains that the Obama administration also refuses to accept the belief that DOMA protects
children and has vowed to work hard to repeal the discriminatory act.*

As you read, consider the following questions:

1. Who is Tracy Schmaler, according to the viewpoint?

2. What are the characteristics of DOMA, as stated in the viewpoint?

3. According to the author, who are Arthur Smelt and Christopher Hammer?

The Obama administration filed court papers Monday claiming a federal marriage law discriminates against gays, even as government lawyers continued to defend it.

Justice Department lawyers are seeking to dismiss a suit brought by a gay California couple challenging the 1996 Defense of Marriage Act. The administration's response to the case has angered gay activists who see it as backtracking on campaign promises made by Barack Obama last year.

In court papers, the administration said it supports repeal of the law.

Yet the same filing says the Justice Department will defend the statute in this case because a reasonable argument can be made that the law is constitutional.

The government's previous filing in the case angered gay rights activists who supported Obama's candidacy in part because of his pledge to move forward on repealing the law and the "don't ask, don't tell" policy that prevents gays from serving openly in the military.

"The administration believes the Defense of Marriage Act is discriminatory and should be repealed," said Justice Department spokeswoman Tracy Schmaler, because it prevents equal rights and benefits.

The department is obligated "to defend federal statutes when they are challenged in court. The Justice Department cannot pick and choose which federal laws it will defend based on any one administration's policy preferences," Schmaler added.

The law, often called DOMA, denies federal recognition of gay marriage and gives states the right to refuse to recognize same-sex marriages performed in other states.

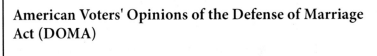

American Voters' Opinions of the Defense of Marriage Act (DOMA)

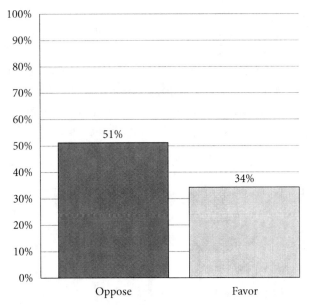

TAKEN FROM: Human Rights Campaign, DOMA Poll 2011, March 8–10, 2011. www.hrc.org.

"DOMA reflects a cautiously limited response to society's still-evolving understanding of the institution of marriage," according to the filing by Assistant Attorney General Tony West.

The administration also disavowed past arguments made by conservatives that DOMA protects children by defining marriage as between a man and a woman.

"The United States does not believe that DOMA is rationally related to any legitimate government interests in procreation and child-rearing and is therefore not relying upon any such interests to defend DOMA's constitutionality," lawyers argued in the filing.

Obama has pledged to work to repeal the law.

Monday's court filing was in response to a lawsuit by Arthur Smelt and Christopher Hammer, who are challenging the federal law, which prevents couples in states that recognize same-sex unions from securing Social Security spousal benefits, filing joint taxes and benefiting from other federal rights connected to marriage.

Justice lawyers have argued that the act is constitutional and contend that awarding federal marriage benefits to gays would infringe on the rights of taxpayers in the 30 states that specifically prohibit same-sex marriages.

Earlier this year, Massachusetts became the first state to challenge the law in court.

Periodical and Internet Sources Bibliography

The following articles have been selected to supplement the diverse views presented in this chapter.

Denny Burk	"Gay Marriage and the Slippery Slope," *Journal for Biblical Manhood & Womanhood*, Fall 2011.
Stephanie Fairyington	"To Wed or Not to Wed," *Progressive*, March 2012.
Benedict Groeschel	"Another Chance to Learn," *Priest*, September 2011.
John Haldane	"Against Erotic Entitlements," *First Things*, April 2012.
Nelson Jones	"Gay Marriage Will Happen—Get Over It," *New Statesman*, March 12, 2012.
Jamie L. Manson	"A Union Made Holy by Love, Faithfulness and Respect," *National Catholic Reporter*, September 12, 2011.
Charles Mum	"Divorce Hypocrisy," *Humanist*, January/February 2012.
Frank Rich	"Whitewashing Gay History," *New York*, February 26, 2012.
Rachel J. Robasciotti	"Marriage: What's It Worth?," *Advocate*, November 17, 2011.
Ron Sider	"Bearing Better Witness," *First Things*, December 2010.
Amy L. Stone	"How the Right Pre-empted Equality," *Gay & Lesbian Review Worldwide*, November/December 2011.
Jacqueline White	"Transgender at the Reunion," *Progressive*, September 2011.

**OPPOSING
VIEWPOINTS®
SERIES**

CHAPTER 3

Should Same-Sex Partners Be Allowed to Adopt?

Chapter Preface

During his political tenure as governor of Massachusetts and his bids for Republican presidential nominee in 2008 and 2012, Mitt Romney argued in favor of a national amendment that would define marriage in America as a union of man and woman. At the same time, Romney insisted that when it comes to the issue of adoption of children by same-sex couples, he believes the states should define their own policies. In his home state, Romney told the *Boston Globe* on March 14, 2006, that same-sex partners have "a legitimate interest in adopting children." However, in an October 2011 town hall meeting in New Hampshire, Romney responded to a question to define his stance on homosexual parenting by stating, "In my view, a society recognizes that the ideal setting for raising a child is when you have the benefit of two people working together and where one is male and one is female."

Romney's various comments on the issue have confused some political commentators as to his true stance, but most have taken him at his word that the states must decide for themselves whether to permit homosexual couples or individuals to adopt children. Some states have very open adoption policies when it comes to gay parents or same-sex partners; others do not. Utah and Mississippi have specific laws prohibiting same-sex partners from adopting, while another handful have statutes that ban second-parent adoption, which is an adoption of a child from a previous marriage or unwed birth, when the new partner is the same sex as the child's parent. Some of those laws and statutes, however, are being challenged in open court. In April 2010, when Arkansas's long-standing ban on gay adoption was ruled unconstitutional, Holly Dickson, a staff attorney with the American Civil Liberties Union, expressed her organization's approval of the judgment. In an article by *On Top* online magazine, Dickson was quoted as stating, "We have a critical shortage of homes now and this ban was denying good, loving homes to our most vulnerable children."

Supporters of adoption by same-sex couples or homosexual individuals often argue that these potential parents just want to take on the family responsibilities and joys unquestionably afforded to most heterosexuals. Many, indeed, have eagerly sought out child rearing in those states that permit gay adoption. According to a report by Kelli Kennedy for the *Huffington Post* on October 20, 2011, "The number of gays and lesbians adopting children has nearly tripled in the past decade." Citing a University of California, Los Angeles law school survey, Kennedy reports that "about 21,740 same-sex couples had an adopted child in 2009, up from 6,477 in 2000." The same article notes that more than 32,500 adopted children were living with same-sex parents in 2009.

Despite the increase in the number of adopted children finding homes, detractors of adoption by same-sex couples follow Romney's reasoning that children thrive better when they have a mother and a father. For example, United Families International (UFI), a public charity that claims no affiliation with a specific religious or political point of view, states that "compared with children from traditional families, children from nontraditional families showed more psychological problems as rated by their parents and more internalizing behavior as rated by their teachers." UFI also cites research that contends children raised by homosexuals are more likely to become homosexuals when compared to children raised by heterosexual couples.

In the chapter that follows, commentators from both sides of the issue weigh in on whether it is appropriate to allow same-sex partners to adopt children. Some of the selected authors also discuss how the states are addressing the issue of parental rights when it comes to homosexual individuals and couples.

"Evidence shows that gay men and lesbians make just as good parents as their heterosexual counterparts, and the public increasingly supports gay adoption rights."

Homosexuals Should Be Allowed to Adopt

Jerome Hunt and Jeffrey Krehely

In the viewpoint that follows, Jerome Hunt and Jeffrey Krehely insist that state laws that bar homosexuals or same-sex couples from adopting children are discriminatory and out of step with the changing times. The authors assert that same-sex parents are as capable of bringing up well-adjusted children in loving homes as heterosexual couples are. Hunt and Krehely believe that public opinion and federal lawmakers have reached the same conclusion, so the time is ripe to overturn remaining antigay adoption policies in the United States. Jeffrey Krehely is vice president of LGBT Research and Communications Project at the Center for American Progress, a research institute that favors progressive ideas in shaping public policy. Jerome Hunt is a research associate at the same institution.

As you read, consider the following questions:

1. Using information from Hunt and Krehely's viewpoint, name two states that have put up legal barriers to same-sex adoption and describe these states' laws as the authors define them.

2. According to the Williams Institute/Urban Institute study, how many children would be removed from foster care homes if a nationwide ban on prohibiting foster care by same-sex couples went into effect?

3. As the authors state, how would the Every Child Deserves a Family Act help fight against adoption-process discrimination based on sexual orientation?

A Florida appeals court unanimously decided last month [September 2010] that a state ban on adoption by gay men and lesbians was unconstitutional (Florida governor Charlie Crist also said that the state will stop enforcing the law). This is a reminder that the struggle for LGBT [lesbian, gay, bisexual, and transgender] equality extends far beyond the headline issues of repealing "Don't Ask, Don't Tell" [a policy that kept homosexual military personnel from revealing their sexual orientation], passing the Employment Non-Discrimination Act, and achieving marriage rights for gay couples.

The victory in Florida is a huge win for advocates of children's rights and well-being as well as those working for LGBT equality. But several states still unfairly target gay men and lesbians who want to adopt or foster children.

These policies should be overturned. They do nothing to serve our nation's foster children and have high economic costs. What's more, evidence shows that gay men and lesbians make just as good parents as their heterosexual counterparts, and the public increasingly supports gay adoption rights.

Current Same-Sex Partner Adoption Policies in the United States

The Family Equality Council finds that only six states have laws or policies that expressly prohibit discrimination against gay and lesbian adoptions (California, Maryland, Massachusetts, Nevada, New Jersey, and New York). The Florida appeals court's ruling now decreases the number of states that expressly restrict adoption by same-sex couples to three—Michigan, Mississippi, and Nebraska.

The Michigan attorney general issued an opinion in 2004 that prevents same-sex couples married in other jurisdictions from adopting children in Michigan. Single gay and lesbian individuals, however, may petition to adopt. The director of Nebraska's Department of Social Services issued a directive in 1995 that prohibits adoption by gay individuals and unmarried, cohabiting individuals. Mississippi, on the other hand, simply prohibits adoption by all same-sex couples.

Three states (North Dakota, Utah, and Arkansas) currently have laws or policies on their books that may effectively restrict adoption by gay men and women. North Dakota allows social workers to make decisions about potential adoptive parents on the basis of their moral or religious convictions. Utah passed two provisions on adoptions in the last 10 years. The first, in 2000, prohibited unmarried cohabiting individuals from adopting. The second, in 2007, gave preference to married heterosexual couples over single adults in placement decisions. Finally, Arkansas prohibits unmarried, cohabitating individuals from adopting.

These states' policies make it nearly impossible for gay men and women to adopt children even if the law doesn't specifically single them out. If a state bars unmarried couples from adopting—and the state doesn't recognize any form of same-sex relationship—then gay people are prohibited from being adoptive parents. Fundamentally, these policies are based on nothing more than antigay bias. They shortchange children who need permanent homes and cost states a lot of money.

The Human and Financial Costs of Restrictive State Policies

These policies equal high costs both in terms of state budget dollars and the number of children affected. The Williams Institute, a legal and policy think tank at the UCLA [University of California, Los Angeles] School of Law, estimates that the Florida ban kept 165 children in foster care, costing the state $2.5 million per year. Williams also estimates that 219 children will be adopted by same-sex couples now that the ban is lifted, saving the state $3.4 million.

The Williams Institute partnered with the Urban Institute to calculate the cost of a nationwide ban on foster care by same-sex couples. They found it would cost somewhere between $87 million to $130 million a year. This ban would also remove an estimated 9,300 and 14,000 children from their current foster homes. Costs to individual states would vary widely based on their share of children in foster care and the adult gay and lesbian population. At the low end of the spectrum, South Dakota would incur $100,000 in costs, while California would be hit with a $27 million bill.

Same-Sex Parents Are Good Parents

Child development experts point out that gay men and lesbians are as good at parenting as their heterosexual peers. Abbie E. Goldberg, in *Lesbian and Gay Parents and Their Children*, finds that same-sex parents are not markedly different from heterosexual parents. Dr. Michael Lamb, a developmental psychologist who provided expert testimony in the Proposition 8 case in California over same-sex marriage, stated during his testimony before the district court that research shows children raised by a gay or lesbian parent are just as likely to grow up well-adjusted adults as children raised by heterosexual par-

States That Permit Joint Adoption by Same-Sex Partners

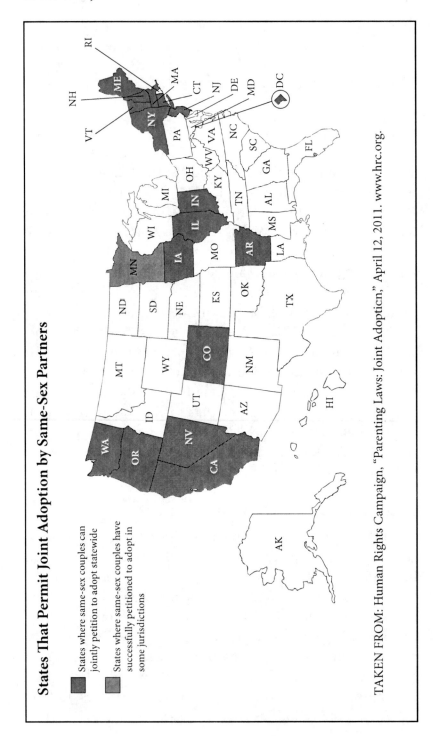

■ States where same-sex couples can jointly petition to adopt statewide

▨ States where same-sex couples have successfully petitioned to adopt in some jurisdictions

TAKEN FROM: Human Rights Campaign, "Parenting Laws: Joint Adoption," April 12, 2011. www.hrc.org.

ents. Similarly, researchers at the University of Virginia find that children adopted by lesbian and gay couples develop no differently than children adopted by heterosexual couples.

Public opinion about gay rights, including adoption rights, is changing. Quinnipiac University conducted a poll of Florida residents in 2009 showing that 55 percent opposed the just-overturned state law that prohibited gay men and lesbians from adopting children. Quinnipiac also conducted a national poll the same year showing 53 percent of Americans support allowing same-sex couples to adopt children.

Further, a Gallup poll reveals a seven-point increase (46 percent to 53 percent) in public support of adoption rights for gay men and lesbians from 2000–2009. And finally, the Public Religion Research Institute finds that the percentage of Americans who think it's bad for society to have gay and lesbian couples raising children declined 14 points from 56 percent in 1997 to 42 percent today.

The Federal Response Is Promising

Some legislators are taking steps to help. Rep. Pete Stark (D-CA) recently introduced the Every Child Deserves a Family Act [in 2009] to help as many children as possible find loving and permanent homes. Stark's bill would prohibit an entity that receives federal assistance and is involved in adoption or foster care placements from discriminating against prospective adoptive or foster parents solely on the basis of their sexual orientation, gender identification, or marital status.

Both child advocacy organizations as well as LGBT equality groups applaud this proposal, including the American Bar Association, Child Welfare League [of America], American Civil Liberties Union [ACLU], American Psychological Association, Family Equality Council, and the Human Rights Campaign.

The American Civil Liberties Union stated in a letter of support:

The goal of our adoption and foster care systems is to provide all children with permanent, stable homes with loving and supportive parents, but discrimination on the basis of sexual orientation, gender identity and marital status hinders that. The [act] will help to ensure that children are not needlessly kept waiting for families because willing and able loving families are being turned away.... The ACLU urges your support for the Every Child Deserves a Family Act.

The American Bar Association echoed similar sentiments when they thanked Representative Stark for "introducing [the Every Child Deserves a Family Act], which will promote permanency for the hundreds of thousands of children waiting in foster care by removing sexual orientation as a bar to child placement decisions when the placement is in the best interest of the child."

Time for These Laws to Go

State policies banning gay men and lesbians from fostering or adopting children hurt everyone involved. State governments bear discrimination's economic costs, same-sex couples are denied the ability to build a family, and, most importantly, children in need of loving and permanent homes are left in unstable caregiving situations.

During a time of state budget crunches it makes no sense to continue these discriminatory policies. Such laws and regulations are based on animus toward gay men and women, not on sound economic or social science. It's time to erase them from the books.

> *"Gays are far too volatile and unstable as a group for society to justify risking the safety of its children."*

Homosexuals Should Not Be Allowed to Adopt

Gregory Rogers

Gregory Rogers is a writer living in South Africa. He writes extensively on subjects of theology and homosexual activism. In the following viewpoint, Rogers maintains that same-sex couples should not be allowed to adopt children. He argues that pro-same-sex adoption research is spotty and inconclusive, while common sense would seem to dictate that children should not be placed in the care of gay and lesbian couples because of obvious hazards. For Rogers, these include the instability of homosexual relationships, evidence of widespread pedophilia within the gay community, and the possible psychological and social problems associated with children reared in homes without a mother and a father. For these reasons, Rogers believes it is wrong to trust homosexual couples with the fragile and impressionable development of children.

Gregory Rogers, "'Suffer the Children': What's Wrong with Gay Adoption?," *Christian Research Journal*, vol. 28, no. 2, 2005. Copyright © 2005 by Christian Research Journal, www.equip.org. All rights reserved. Adapted with permission.

As you read, consider the following questions:

1. What does Rogers say was the outcome of the American Academy of Pediatrics endorsement of gay adoption in 2002?

2. What evidence does Rogers use to support his claim that both father and mother play a pivotal role in child development?

3. How does Rogers refute the argument that tolerating same-sex adoption would mean a significant increase in the number of prospective parents available to adopt?

> We [gay and lesbian activists] have been on the defensive too long. It's time to affirm that the Right is correct in some of its pronouncements about our movement. [Conservative political commentator] Pat Buchanan said there was a "cultural war" going on "for the soul of America" and that gay and lesbian rights were the principal battleground. He was right. Similarly, [homo]'phobes like [television evangelist] Pat Robertson are right when they say that we threaten the family, male domination, and the Calvinist ethic of work and grimness that has paralyzed most Americans' search for pleasure. Indeed, instead of proclaiming our innocuousness, we ought to advertise our potential to change straight society in radical, beneficial ways. . . . Pleasure is possible (and desirable) beyond the sanction of the state.
>
> —*Lesbian activist Donna Minkowitz*

It is difficult to avoid the thought that if the above pronouncement had been made some 30 years earlier, public dignity never would have stood for it, and a Western world based on Judeo-Christian principles would have proudly resisted. The gay lobby has made such strides in recent decades as can only be called daunting. Beginning with the claim to right of lifestyle behind closed doors, they have progressed to demanding the consent of society's *doctors* regarding sex change operations, of society's *media* regarding gay-oriented films and television shows, and of society's *laws* regarding same-sex marriage. Finally, they want society's *children*.

Legal and political bodies around the world already have sanctioned legal adoption of children by homosexuals. According to some, such decisions rest on reliable scientific evidence and sure ethical foresight. According to others, however, such decisions lack sufficient basis, and those who made them have eschewed the truth for political correctness and the new doctrine of tolerance.

As the controversy moves to crisis point, one may well discover that what is at stake is not merely the welfare of children—though this is serious enough—but the foundation of the Judeo-Christian West itself.

The Ongoing Debate over Same-Sex Adoption

Gay activists have been quick to promote their agenda in political and psychiatric circles, bringing pressure to bear on the relevant authorities. Their successes have been few but sure, and popular impression is that they may well achieve victory in this arena before long.

Gay interests received a boost in February 2002, when the American Academy of Pediatrics (AAP) announced that it would support adoption by gays in the future. The decision, however, did not go unchallenged. Many clinicians, including more than 600 members of the AAP, walked out of the academy in protest.

In a recent [2004] decision, the Eleventh Circuit Court of Appeals upheld the prevailing Florida position against same-sex adoption. The court argued that "the state's overriding interest is not providing individuals the opportunity to become parents, but rather identifying those individuals whom it deems most capable of parenting adoptive children and providing them with a secure family environment." An increasing number of states have found in favor of gay adoption in the United States, however.

The force of the debate also has been felt elsewhere. In Denmark child custody rights have been awarded to gay couples, with similar rights being granted by Canadian courts.

It is clear, then, that we are poised on the brink of an unprecedented legal and ethical battle. Only the future will tell what ground the courts and governments of the world may or may not concede to the gay lobby.

Questionable Role Models

One of the first questions raised in the matter of adoption pertains to the emotional and psychological well-being of the potential parents. There is a plethora of studies that indicate the extreme emotional and sexual instability of many gays and lesbians in this regard.

According to a recent study of gay relationships reported in the *Journal of Sex Research*, "The modal range for number of sexual partners ever was 101–500." Some 10.2 percent to 15.7 percent reported between 501 and 1,000 partners, with a further 10.2 percent to 15.7 percent having had over 1,000 in the course of their lives.

The stability of gay relationships can also be questioned. Prominent gay activist (and same-sex marriage advocate) Andrew Sullivan speaks glowingly of infidelity in same-sex unions, in that

> same-sex unions often incorporate the virtues of friendship more effectively than traditional marriages; and at times, among gay male relationships, the openness of the contract makes it more likely to survive than many heterosexual bonds. . . . There is more likely to be greater understanding of the need for extramarital outlets between two men than between a man and a woman. But something of the gay

relationship's necessary honesty, its flexibility, and its equality could undoubtedly help strengthen and inform many heterosexual bonds.

Figures for suicidal tendencies are also unacceptably high. A recent study reported in the *American Journal of Public Health* revealed that gay people are six times more likely to attempt suicide than are straights.

Worse still, there is evidence of high levels of domestic violence within gay households. Gay authors [David] Island and [Patrick] Letellier admit in their book *Men Who Beat the Men Who Love Them: Battered Gay Men and Domestic Violence* that "the incidence of domestic violence among gay men is nearly double that in the heterosexual population."

One wonders what sort of impact such an environment will have on the mind and emotional well-being of a child. Further, could that child become the recipient of the domestic violence—or even promiscuity—in question?

Some have objected that "gay angst" is due to "societal homophobia," and that as soon as homosexuality is fully endorsed by society, such emotional problems will dissipate. This, however, cannot be conclusively proven by science, and there is evidence that gay angst in fact has more to do with homosexuality as an innate condition. Research scientist Neil Whitehead reviewed several studies whose evidence indicated that societal attitudes appeared to make no difference, and that gay angst is just as prevalent in liberal gay-tolerant countries as it is elsewhere in the world.

The Pedophilia Problem

The connection between homosexuality and pedophilia has long haunted the public consciousness. In response, the gay lobby—as well as important bodies such as the American Psychological Association (APA)—insist that there is no evidence that gays commit pedophilia at a higher rate than do straights.

The argument runs that, on a hand count, cases of heterosexual pedophilia outnumber those of homosexual pedophilia; however, as Yale and Harvard-connected psychiatrist Jeffrey Satinover points out,

> Careful studies show that pedophilia is far more common among homosexuals than heterosexuals. The greater absolute number of heterosexual cases reflects the fact that heterosexual males outnumber homosexual males by approximately thirty-six to one. Heterosexual child molestation cases outnumber homosexual cases by only eleven to one, implying that pedophilia is more than three times more common among homosexuals.

Space does not permit a deeper treatment of the subject, except to say that subsequent scientific arguments have been proposed elsewhere, and that the subject needs more scientific research. What is clear is that the idea that there is no significant link between homosexuality and pedophilia is by no means settled among clinicians, regardless of the official statements of various authoritative bodies.

What is clearer, and needs to be brought to the fore—with some urgency—is that the literature of the gay subculture contains an alarming frequency of open references to pedophilia and child molestation. The *Journal of Homosexuality* (whose editor, John De Cecco, also sits on the editorial board of the pedophilia advocacy journal *Paedika*) ran a double issue in 1990 that was devoted entirely to "male intergenerational intimacy." As Satinover points out,

> This special issue reflects the substantial, influential, and growing segment of the homosexual community that neither hides nor condemns pedophilia. Rather they argue that pedophilia is an acceptable aspect of sexuality, *especially of homosexuality*. Indeed, the *San Francisco Sentinel*, a Bay Area gay-activist newspaper, published a piece arguing that pedophilia is central to the male homosexual life (emphasis in original).

Orphaned Children Should Not Be Placed in Unstable Homes

Because children surrendered for adoption have already suffered one major loss, it is very important that they be placed in the most stable situation possible. Same-sex couples are the least stable arrangement.

Gay male couples are very likely to break up; even if they remain together, they are rarely sexually faithful to one another. Lesbian couples are more likely to remain together than gay male couples, but they are not nearly as stable as married heterosexual couples.

Dale O'Leary,
"Dangers of Same-Sex Couples Adopting Children (Part 2),"
Zenit, November 5, 2004. www.zenit.org.

The unabashed international campaigns of the gay lobby to lower the age of sexual consent are also noteworthy. From as early as 1972, the National Coalition of Gay Organizations included among their aims the "repeal of all laws governing the age of sexual consent," in some countries to as low as 14 years. . . .

An Unbalanced Family

One cannot ignore the fact that for a child to develop to emotional and psychological maturity it is preferable that both mother and father be present. Each party makes a different but vital contribution to that child's welfare.

According to researcher Henry Biller, "Differences between the mother and father can be very stimulating to the infant, even those that might appear quite superficial to the adult. Even if the father and mother behave in generally similar ways, they provide contrasting images for the infant."

Sociologist David Popenoe observes,

> Through their play, as well as in their other child-rearing activities, fathers tend to stress competition, challenge, initiative, risk taking, and independence. Mothers in their caretaking roles, in contrast, stress emotional security and personal safety.... While mothers provide ... important flexibility and sympathy in their discipline, fathers provide ultimate predictability and consistency. Both dimensions are critical for ... efficient, balanced, and humane child rearing.

Studies have shown that fatherless children are twice as likely to become school dropouts, are significantly more likely to become victims of alcohol and drug abuse, and are 4.3 times more likely to smoke than children growing up with fathers. Few studies have been conducted on motherless homes, presumably because of their sparsity, but one study indicates that motherless homes are 56 percent more likely to produce daughters who experience teen pregnancy.

Nor can it be argued that the statistics relate to single parents in general rather than to an absent father or mother situation as such. The fact (as demonstrated above) is that both father and mother play a pivotal role in the child's development, with both needed to provide balanced upbringing. Absence of either will many times result in confusion and identity malformation. This is the case in any single-gender parent family, whether gay or straight. Further, single-parent families in society are widely regarded as second best, evolving out of necessity rather than the ideal option. As long as we keep our eyes on this, we have a balanced perspective. What the gay argument actually does is insist that we accept single-gender gay parenting as "just another healthy alternative," when this is not the case.

Undermining the "Good Parents" Studies

Contrary to the expectations of many, since their inception, circa 1970, gay-parenting studies have been almost unanimous in their *official* findings that there are "no notable differences between children reared by heterosexual parents and those reared by lesbian and gay parents," and in finding lesbian and gay parents "to be as competent and effective as heterosexual parents."

Social science researchers Robert Lerner and Althea Nagai, however, produced a 2001 survey that challenged the above contention. The work, entitled "No Basis: What the Studies Don't Tell Us About Same-Sex Parenting," surveyed 49 of the most prominent studies conducted to date, dismissing all without exception as of limited use at best.

According to Lerner and Nagai, "the methods used in these studies are so flawed that these studies prove nothing. Therefore, they should not be used in legal cases to make any argument about 'homosexual vs. heterosexual' parenting. Their claims have no basis."

Their work postulated several basic traits of a good survey and demonstrated how all 49 hopelessly failed to match these criteria. Of the 49, it accused 18 of "undue partiality," and found 21 not to have a "heterosexual comparison group" with which to compare the homosexual group in question, making confident comparison difficult. . . .

Answering Some Objections

In response to the above, an APA publication argues, "In the long run, it is not the results obtained from any one specific sample, but the accumulation of findings from many different samples that will be most meaningful." What this is actually saying, however, is that we should be prepared to risk the safety and well-being of our children for the sake of inconclusive, and much misrepresented, research, a factor doubtless influenced by the presence of gay clinicians as well as a politically correct mind-set.

Many governments of the world have condemned human cloning, by comparison, because of, among other things, potentially detrimental emotional and psychological consequences for those who would be cloned. If we can prohibit cloning with no prior studies conducted on clone subjects, based simply on common sense and fear of what *might* happen, how much more should we refrain from experimenting on our children, for fear of similar consequences? No run of inadequate studies will make up for the lives that would be damaged if we are wrong.

Some people may raise the objection that because the tests are inconclusive, reliable studies need to be conducted as soon as possible. One then can counter by inquiring as to whose children we are to use as guinea pigs. We are dealing with a group in which gross promiscuity, pedophilia, AIDS, suicide, and instability are known factors. The suggestion appears to be one more likely entertained in a barbarous rather than a civilized culture.

Others may raise the further point that gay adoption can do much to alleviate the substantial orphan problem, not only in America, but in the rest of the world, and that same-sex couples can serve to increase the number of prospective parents for those orphans. The most reliable recent figures, however, place the occurrence of homosexuality in society at around two percent. Taking into account, moreover, that not all gays are going to adopt, and that even fewer would probably be judged fit parents, the number of orphans who would be cared for seems fairly negligible.

It is important to recognize, further, that the highest good, or the child's best interest, is not necessarily *having parents*, but *having well-being* itself. The two do not necessarily amount to the same thing. We would be loath, for example, to grant a child to a known pedophile simply for the sake of supplying a parent figure. In light of the aforementioned data, we must face the very real possibility that having children growing up in same-sex homes may exacerbate rather than resolve the problem. To put it another way: Adoption does not solve all ills. There are cases in which the lesser of two evils is for the child to have no parent. There exists the very real possibility that gay parenthood may in fact add to, and not detract from, the angst of the orphan.

The conservative position will doubtless be accused of intolerance and discrimination. In response, one may inquire: intolerant of and discriminatory against whom, the *gay parents* or the *children*?

As the Eleventh Circuit Court pointed out in their recent decision supporting the Florida ban on gay adoption, "In Florida, adoption is not a right, but a statutory privilege." Those who cry "rights" demonstrate a failure of priorities—and therefore of the requisite sense of responsibility in this matter. As the former British Home Secretary Jack Straw points out, "We should not see children as trophies."

This brings us to the next important point. Adoption of children has been touted as a gay rights issue, and even, in a recent case involving adoption by lesbians, a women's rights issue. This, however, misses the point entirely. When we come to the matter of adoption of children, it is always first and foremost a *children's rights issue*. In the frantic cry for "rights" over privilege, the rights of the children often do not seem to be considered. . . .

With the failings—and bias—of gay-parenting studies, we have to conclude that we simply do not have sufficient scientific basis to condone gay adoption. We do have sufficient basis, however, to determine that gays are far too volatile and unstable as a group for society to justify risking the safety of its children. Consider the group's significantly higher rates of suicidal tendency, promiscuity, pedophilia, and domestic violence. This does not even touch the possible negative impact children may suffer simply from having two parents of the same sex. Is society really willing to risk its fragile children for the sake of politics?

What is being proposed by the gay lobby is not just another single-parent family or adoption situation, but an *all-new family unit*, consisting of a mother-and-mother with children or a father-and-father with children. This is something the likes of which the Judeo-Christian ethic has not heard, nor has the West, which rests on this ethic. The family is the building block of society. When the building block of society falls, society falls with it. What is under threat here is not simply the well-being of children—which is important enough—it is the fabric of Western society itself.

"It is not possible to discriminate against prospective [gay, lesbian, bisexual, and transgender] parents, without also showing utter disrespect for the thousands of kids who need them so desperately."

Same-Sex Adoption Should Be Supported for the Sake of Encouraging Adoption

Kerry Hosking

In the following viewpoint, Kerry Hosking, a psychology and metaphysics student, claims that the number of children waiting to be adopted exceeds the number of heterosexual people willing to adopt. She asserts, then, that it is logical to allow gay and lesbian individuals as well as same-sex couples to be added to the pool of prospective parents. She maintains that homosexual households statistically have sufficient income to foster children and could relieve the financial burden that the federal and state governments must assume to care for orphaned children. Beyond this logic, though, Hosking insists that attempts to ban homosexuals from adopting are purely driven by prejudice that does not have the best interests of the children at heart. She argues that objections raised on religious or any other grounds must be overcome in order to provide stable, loving homes for the numerous children hoping to be adopted.

As you read, consider the following questions:

1. According to Hosking, how much money would the government have to spend on child care if there were a national ban on GLBT adoption?

2. As the author states, why did the Arkansas Family Council inadvertently have to promote the banning of adoption by prospective single-parent heterosexuals?

3. Why does Hosking find it necessary to state that the American Psychological Association does not recognize homosexuality as a mental deficiency?

For the sake of many thousands of children in state-funded facilities, the issue of gay adoption must be resolved using logic and not biased opinion. Many would argue that two-parent heterosexual families can provide a child with a more stable upbringing. This solution would certainly reduce the number of beautiful children who are in need of loving homes, but reality clearly shows that the number of heterosexual couples is exceeded by the number of children who patiently wait for them.

Although many would argue that gay adoption is inappropriate, and contradictory to many religious beliefs, the number of children needing to be placed with these loving families is steadily increasing; therefore, laws should be amended to allow same-sex adoption. In the United States, state laws vary on the issue of gay, lesbian, bisexual and transgender adoption (GLBT). At this time, only a handful of states permit GLBT adoption, or same-sex joint adoption. For economic reasons as well as logic, the inevitable burden to the taxpayer is also steadily on the rise. For instance, a national ban on GLBT adoption could see the federal government facing a $130 million expense to take care of children who could have already been placed into families. Figures from the Census Bureau [in 2008] show that "the percentage of adopted children under 18 who are black is 16%. Additionally, 7 percent are Asian and 2 percent are American Indian and Alaska native. Adopted children are more likely to be of these race groups than are biological children or stepchildren."

Finding More Adoptive Parents

The only economic solution appears to be the most obvious; that is, to locate as many new adoptive parents as possible to raise these beautiful children. But where does one begin the search for such people? Many heterosexual couples, who are already raising families of their own, opt to adopt children, though many only adopt one child. Some families prefer to adopt a child who is the same race as they are; some have not given any thought to adoption or fostering a child at all. Is there any method of advertising effective enough to prompt prospective parents to adopt? If not, it would appear that numbers of orphaned children will continue to rise, as the number of families wanting to provide them with homes steadily decreases. In the state of Arkansas alone, "the Senate moved to ban gay couples from adopting or fostering children. However, a study on the economic effects of gay adoption found that 9,300 to 14,000 children would be displaced if gay couples were expelled from the foster and adoptive care systems" [according to David Weigel in the July 2007 issue of Reason].

There are plenty of same-sex couples willing to adopt or foster children, and this would provide a simple solution to decreasing the number of children who are in state care facilities and foster homes. When it comes to locating these generous and loving families, Arkansas seems to be one state which has repeatedly taken backward steps. The Arkansas Family Council has been actively pursuing a ban on unmarried couples fostering or adopting children. In the state of Arkansas, gay couples cannot be married, nor are they recognized as married if the union took place in another state or country. Ironically, to put such a ban into place, this group of advocates has also had to ban heterosexual single parents. This significantly adds to the already present problem of too many children and not enough eligible adoptive families.

Bans Are Unacceptable

In 2008, it was reported that Arkansas voters would decide whether to ban unmarried couples from fostering or adopting children. Secretary of State Charlie Daniels certified the measure, saying that the Arkansas Family Council Action Committee had submitted 85,389 valid signatures from registered voters—more than 23,000 more valid names than required by law. Last month [in February 2009] the socially conservative group that spearheaded Arkansas's constitutional ban on same-sex marriage handed in its petitions prior to the state deadline for getting issues on the November ballot. But the secretary of state validated only 57,888 signatures. Since the number fell within a state "grace" guideline the group was given another 30 days to get the additional signatures.

Arkansas Families First, the group fighting the measure said it is preparing to take the issue to court. Spokesperson Debbie Willhite said the group will ask the Arkansas Supreme Court to enjoin the initiative. The adoption referendum is similar to a bill that died in the legislature earlier this year. That legislation failed after Gov. Mike Beebe suggested that there were constitutional problems with the bill, although he would not say if he intended to veto it if it were passed.

Update: Arkansas voters have opted to ban the adoption and foster care of children by "single parents," a devious move to exclude those who are gay. Now what?

Of the escalating number of children needing to be adopted, it should also be noted that many children can only be adopted along with their siblings. In addition to this, over 500,000 children awaiting adoption in these United States are African American boys. Based on common sense it is also easy to see that the number of African American parents waiting to adopt children is significantly lower than the number of white heterosexual couples. Taking all of these variables into account, it can safely be said that any ban which limits the number of eligible parents to foster or adopt is simply unacceptable. Reports by Fox News and the Associated Press (2008) recently quoted Dr. Jill Fussell, a pediatrician, who said, "We need more homes, not less."

Stable Incomes and Stable Lives

Still on the topic of economics, no evidence has been presented to suggest that a white heterosexual couple is more financially stable than any same-sex couple. In fact, the opposite is the case, with statistics showing that "significantly, same-sex couples raising adopted children are older, more educated, and have more economic resources than other adoptive parents. This is fortunate for the foster care system because an estimated 14,000 foster children are living with lesbian or gay parents, which means that same-sex parents are raising three percent of foster children in America" [according to Lynne Maxwell in an April 2008 issue of *Library Journal*]. So what is the fate of these thousands of babies if a ban is put into place? Will there be enough white heterosexual couples who are financially able and emotionally willing to adopt? The answer is of course, a resounding no, regardless of the presence of all biased opinion about homosexuality. It is a simple assumption that if no other solution is found and religious organizations cannot offer an unbiased alternative to this ongoing crisis, logic simply must prevail.

The American Psychological Association does not recognize the presence of any mental deficiency where same-sex, homosexual or lesbian parents are concerned. In fact, homosexuality is not even on the list of diagnosable disorders. Biased opinion using mental stability is commonly the product of ignorance and prejudice, and therefore it has no place in the process of implementing legislation. A greater concern should be that of eradicating acts of discrimination. After all, it is not the case that African American couples are not permitted to adopt children; the GLBT community deserves the same privileges as anyone else. Furthermore, such discrimination toward these groups of people directly affects the future of every child in state care, but does little to deter these devoted would-be parents. It is not possible to discriminate against prospective GLBT parents without also showing utter disrespect for the thousands of kids who need them so desperately.

Religious Objections Leave Children Out in the Cold

Respect is also due to those whose religious beliefs do not condone homosexuality. In an article concerning discrimination published in *Christianity Today*, "There is no wish to discriminate against gay people in service provision," said Don Horrocks, the Evangelical Alliance's head of public affairs. "Rather, Christians and other religious groups don't want to find themselves coerced by law to facilitate or promote homosexual activity. It involves a basic religious liberty freedom of conscience." It should also be noted, however, that such actions also cross the line where privacy issues are concerned, once again leaving the kids out in the cold.

Former British prime minister Tony Blair made his stance on discrimination quite clear in 2007, when he ruled that "Roman Catholic adoption agencies should not be exempted." Despite the ruling though, the Roman Catholic Church warned of its decision to cease placing children into any homes, let alone those of GLBT parents. Ironically, during the ongoing debates over GLBT adoption, no gay person has objected to any religious beliefs which imply that intimate relations must be kept between heterosexual couples, because they see that the issue is not relevant to the needs of the children.

Modern law says that discrimination is not permitted in a workplace environment; therefore, it can also be said that it is hypocritical for anyone to pass judgment about the morals of prospective parents based on their own religious or homophobic opinions. The same can be said for schools, where more needs to be done to implement antiharassment policies. Unfortunately, it is not always the children who are to blame for harassment and discrimination in schools. The American Civil Liberties Union reports that "in spite of this progress, many GLBT youth face tremendous difficulties when they go to school every day. Harassment is commonplace—nearly 70% of GLBT students say they have been harassed, threatened, or physically assaulted at school. And schools themselves are often part of the problem—53% of students say they've heard homophobic comments made by school staff." It is worth restating now that it is logical to allow books about homosexuality in all public and school libraries in an attempt to defeat ignorance.

The Pain of Discrimination

Social workers, too, should be educated sufficiently to be able to offer an unbiased opinion when it comes to recommending or denying prospective parents. Sadly, this is not always the case. Tony Scott and Scott Amos of Tennessee were fortunate to adopt the infant son of a friend, after a social worker recommended them as suitable parents. The social worker, however, was not initially convinced that their home was the right place for the baby and was opposed to the idea for several months. Having spent time with them, she soon changed her mind, and happily, the couple proceeded to adopt the baby's two other siblings as well. Scott and Amos, as well as five of the 18 children they had fostered over the years, had been left heartbroken 11 months earlier when Judge Carey Garrett ordered the removal of the children from their home. The judge made the order after he decided that . . . Amos and Scott's lifestyle was immoral. Another Christian judge, Andrew McClintock, was himself forced to resign from his employment, after being faced with a case where his own bias would interfere with his decision to pass legal judgment.

Discrimination has no place in society for any reason, just as it is not tolerated in the workplace. The sexual preferences of consenting adults have no relevance to the alarming statistics which show the many precious children whose only wish it is to have a place to call home. A proactive approach to creating public awareness will play a major role in removing ignorance and resolving one of the nation's largest ongoing problems. Support for homosexual, gay and lesbian people who are willing and able to make a lifelong commitment to raising healthy and productive families is long overdue. It is clear to all who possess common sense that laws do, indeed, need to be amended to allow GLBT fostering and adoption. For anyone who feels they have a valid reason to oppose such bans, one needs to ask the pertinent question: Are you a foster parent?

"'Tolerance' isn't possible where truth—or reasonable belief—is intentionally suppressed."

Same-Sex Adoption Should Not Be Tolerated for the Sake of Encouraging Adoption

Andrew Haines

Andrew Haines is the chairman of the membership of Ethika Politika, *a web journal of the Center for Morality in Public Life, a collective that believes human integrity and the common good are principles furthered by sound reasoning. In the viewpoint that follows, Haines argues that if it is reasonable to object to gay adoption on the basis that homosexuality is a bad lifestyle choice, then it is unacceptable to ask those who advocate this position to relinquish it to create a "situational good," namely a potential increase in the number of adoptions. Haines believes that encouraging adoption is not sufficient reason to require those who hold that homosexuality is wrong to tolerate same-sex adoption.*

As you read, consider the following questions:

1. Why does Haines believe it is inconsequential whether readers agree or disagree with his personal attitudes toward homosexuality or same-sex marriage?

2. Why does Haines believe that it also does not matter in his logical argument whether homosexual people are good-hearted in their desire to adopt?

3. On what issue relating to gay rights does Haines believe there is no middle ground?

The title of this post ["Is Gay Adoption Worth Tolerating?"] already lets on to one big presupposition: that adoption by gay couples shouldn't be endorsed. But the question I want to ask is, should we tolerate it?

Let's get the obvious concerns out of the way first. A few readers might agree with me that gay adoption is *not* a good thing. And they might agree with me for a number of reasons—perhaps because it contributes to a deformation of the family, or because it presumes (falsely) an equivalence in the character of heterosexual versus homosexual relationships.

Many will probably disagree with me. That's okay. This post has more to do with "tolerance" than the status of homosexual relationships, anyway. (And who doesn't like talking about tolerance, after all?)

Examining the "Greater Good" Argument

Imagine—for the sake of argument—that gay marriage is not okay. In fact, it's wrong. Imagine that it's tantamount to killing baby seals for their pelts or succumbing to the abysmal cultural bias toward sexual mononormativity. You know, things that are *really* and unwaveringly wrong.

Now, in this world—much like the one we live in—suppose there are also a tremendous number of unfortunate orphans, being shoved throughout the foster care system. Imagine that a great many of them are disillusioned, depressed, and want nothing more than a loving home and caring parents.

In this world—let's call it "Reality"—there's a strong push to do anything (reasonably) possible to get the greatest number of orphans out of foster care and into permanent, loving, and stable homes. It's a common good that everyone agrees on (because in Reality, unlike in our world, people agree on almost everything).

One thing that's not so clear for Real citizens, though, is whether or not *any* loving, caring environment for children is a sufficiently loving and caring one. In other words, do "love" and "care" from parents alone suffice to make a family environment "loving" and "caring?" (In Reality, this is an incredibly difficult distinction.)

Also, in the Real world, despite a vast outcry against it, gay couples have secured the right to get married and adopt children.

For inhabitants of our make-believe place, then, the complexity of the adoption quandary is this: There are many children who would benefit greatly from being adopted; and there are many couples legally able to adopt them; but some of those couples are caught up in bad lifestyle choices; and a subset of *those* couples are homosexual. (Remember, it's wrong.)

The problem plaguing a lot of Real folks is the fact that gay couples, while clearly a segment of the "bad lifestyle" group, aren't necessarily the sort that deal drugs and engage in domestic violence. In fact, many of them have good jobs, stable incomes, demonstrate genuine compassion, and would do almost anything to give the best possible care to a child in their custody. In short, they're good-hearted people.

The problem, of course, is that they're still a subset of the "bad lifestyle" sort. And "bad lifestyle" (across the board) certainly translates to "unfit for child rearing."

So although the citizens of Reality would never (and could never ethically) *endorse* adoption by gay couples, is it something they should be willing to tolerate?

End scenario.

Sacrificing a Reasonable Belief Is Unwarranted

Certainly, no one's views on the defensibility of gay marriage have changed. You're still where you were two minutes ago, right? Good.

But thanks for playing my game, because there's a question here that needs to be answered: Namely, is it justifiable for people firmly committed to a basic truth (or reasonable belief) to lay it aside in favor of advancing another, situational good?

This is a dilemma that we should all feel comfortable facing, because it's ubiquitous. For the Realists (and for a great number of Americans), it's a problem of setting aside incoherent lifestyle choices for the sake of a commonly acknowledged societal benefit. But in general, it's a problem of surrendering rationally held ground for the sake of advancing a different, yet equally rationally motivated benefit.

The problem, of course, is that rational truth doesn't contradict itself.

In our world, free from the blasé conformity of Reality, the adoption dilemma plays out with rather more convolution. By and large, though, it takes the form of gay rights advocates demanding that their opponents back down from barring homosexual couples from adopting—in effect, a demand to sacrifice a reasonably held belief for the sake of a reasonable, situational good. On the flip side, there are antigay rights advocates who don't see the harm in backing off, "as long as it's good for the kids."

Unfortunately, neither position addresses the real question at stake. And it's about time we stop lying to ourselves. Any issue of gay rights is a matter of basic principles—namely, the principle that either justifies or annihilates the value of gay marriage. There's no middle ground. There's no holding firm on one front while backing off on the other. There can't be.

"Tolerance" isn't possible where truth—or reasonable belief—is intentionally suppressed. And the time has come to stop asking for it.

Periodical and Internet Sources Bibliography

The following articles have been selected to supplement the diverse views presented in this chapter.

Vicki Angeline Dennis   "I Did It My Way," *Off Our Backs*, March 2006.

Todd Flowerday   "Children First: How the Church Should Advocate Adoption," *Commonweal*, November 20, 2009.

Serena Lambert   "Gay and Lesbian Families: What We Know and Where to Go from Here," *Family Journal*, January 2005.

Timothy F. Murphy   "Same-Sex Marriage: Not a Threat to Marriage or Children," *Journal of Social Philosophy*, Fall 2011.

Tim Padgett   "Gay Family Values," *Time*, July 5, 2007.

Amanda Ruggeri   "A Quiet Fight over Gay Adoption," *US News & World Report*, November 3, 2008.

Jacob Sullum   "Gay by Force," *Reason*, March 2009.

Alyson Taub   "Fit or Unfit? Homosexuality and Parenting," *Journal of Contemporary Legal Issues*, vol. 16, no. 1, 2007.

Cynthia G. Wagner   "Homosexuality and Family Formation," *Futurist*, May/June 2010.

Misty Wall   "Hearing the Voices of Lesbian Women Having Children," *Journal of GLBT Family Studies*, vol. 7, no. 1–2, 2011.

David Weigel   "Foster Follies," *Reason*, July 2007.

OPPOSING
VIEWPOINTS®
SERIES

CHAPTER 4

Should Homosexuals Be Excluded from Certain Organizations?

Chapter Preface

In 2006 the Family Research Council (FRC), a Christian organization promoting traditional family values, published a pamphlet detailing its arguments against allowing gay-straight alliances on school campuses. The FRC maintains that protecting anyone from harassment is a function of safe schools, but "to raise an entire new generation of young people who will have an unquestioning acceptance of pro-homosexual dogma" should not be part of a school's duties. The FRC cites several examples of school boards and parents discovering that a "pro-homosexual" agenda had been quietly slipped into school curricula and related educational activities in the name of promoting unity. "In North Carolina," the FRC notes, one set of parents were "shocked to learn that the North Carolina Governor's School, an elite state-funded summer program attended by their son, had featured a seminar on 'The New Gay Teenager' that encouraged students to question their own sexuality and biblical teaching against homosexuality." To redress this perceived agenda, the FRC states that parents have the right to speak out against such activities and to oppose gay-straight alliances on campuses and that students who oppose pro-homosexual rhetoric have the right to join gay-straight organizations and speak their minds.

While the FRC does not stipulate that gay, lesbian, bisexual, and transgender (GLBT) children should be denied education, the organization insists that homosexual students and teachers do not have the right to force others to accept the "rightness" of their lifestyle in an educational setting. Gay-straight alliances and their supporters, however, contend that their clubs spread awareness of homophobic harassment and build camaraderie to stress the humanity and dignity of this minority population. The Safe Schools Coalition attests on its website that its membership is commonly open to "straight allies (heterosexual students with a GLBT friend or family member or who just care about the issue)" but that "some [GLBT support groups] restrict membership, for safety's sake, to people who are, or who think they might be, sexual minorities." The FRC argues that homosexual clubs or gay-straight alliances should not have the right to restrict membership and that people with dissenting views about homosexuality should be able to attend and voice their opinions.

Whether GLBT students have a right to form exclusive clubs or whether school boards and parents have the power to keep gay-straight alliances from forming are the subject of debate across America. In the following chapter, several observers offer opinions on whether other institutions in the United States have the authority to bar homosexuals or limit the disclosure of their identities.

| "I have never met a single senior non-commissioned officer in any service who said to me anything like: 'We need some homosexuals and lesbians out here to help us accomplish our mission.'"

Tolerating Open Homosexuality in the Military Will Hurt Unit Effectiveness

Oliver North

Author and political commentator Oliver North is a retired lieutenant colonel in the US Marine Corps. He is the founder and honorary chairman of the Freedom Alliance, an organization that supports military service and promotes national defense. In the following viewpoint, North laments Congress's reconsideration of government policy that keeps homosexuals from serving openly in the military. According to North, military leaders believe gays serving openly in the military would hurt unit morale, especially in the current wartime climate, and many servicepersons have expressed their antipathy toward serving with homosexuals. North fears that repealing the ban on homosexuals serving in the military might influence many fine soldiers to leave the ranks and discourage others from enlisting.

Oliver North, "Gays in the Military," *National Review Online*, December 7, 2010. www.nationalreview.com.

As you read, consider the following questions:

1. As North writes, what part of the US Code adopted in 1993 maintained that service persons who "demonstrate a propensity or intent to engage in homosexual acts" would create an unacceptable risk to military effectiveness?

2. According to the Pentagon's Comprehensive Review Working Group, what percentage of service persons deployed overseas believe that a repeal of the ban on homosexuals serving openly in the military would have a negative impact on combat effectiveness?

3. According to North's reading of the secretary of defense's implementation plan for the new law following the repeal of the ban, what will be denied to service personnel who, by conscientious objection, would ask to leave the military instead of serving with homosexuals?

Adm. Mike Mullen, chairman of the Joint Chiefs of Staff, made a startling statement in congressional testimony last week [on December 2, 2010]. When asked if allowing open homosexuals into the U.S. military would lead to a mass exodus of troops from active service, he boldly declared that they can "find another place to work."

Such a cavalier response to a U.S. senator's serious inquiry may play well in the press and in the current commander in chief's office, but it illuminates a deeply misguided commitment to political correctness and foreshadows serious adverse consequences for our national security. If tens of thousands of troops now serving in the finest military force the world has ever known vote with their feet in the midst of a war, we're all in deep trouble.

At issue is a pending vote in the Senate on repealing Section 654 of Title X of the U.S. Code [USC]. This law, on the books since 1993, states: "The presence in the armed forces of persons who demonstrate a propensity or intent to engage in homosexual acts would create an unacceptable risk to the high standards of morale, good order and discipline, and unit cohesion that are the essence of military capability."

The Dangerous Push to Overturn "Don't Ask, Don't Tell"

President [Barack] Obama describes this "ban on gays" as "unfair" and has vowed, as he put it, to "end 'Don't ask, don't tell.'" Though nothing has happened in the last 17 years to mitigate the "unacceptable risk" to our military, he is supported in this quest to fulfill a campaign promise by Defense Secretary Robert Gates and the Joint Chiefs chairman, Admiral Mullen. The House of Representatives has already voted to repeal Section 654. Now it's the Senate's turn to consider the question.

For the record, the phrase "don't ask, don't tell" appears nowhere in the actual law. It's simply a policy adopted by the [President Bill] Clinton administration as a way of avoiding a confrontation with Congress [by suggesting that homosexual service members keep their sexual orientation to themselves]—and a public relations disaster with the far-left wing of the American body politic. Repeal by the present lame-duck Congress would overturn not just the informal "don't ask, don't tell" policy, but the statutory prohibition on open homosexual men and lesbians in the ranks.

According to Messrs. Obama, Gates, and Mullen—and "GLBT [gay, lesbian, bisexual, and transgender] rights" activists—the report of the Comprehensive Review Working Group, released by the Pentagon on November 30, finds that there is "low risk" to unit cohesion and military readiness in immediately repealing the law. But a careful reading of the report suggests otherwise.

Another Factor That Will Impair Military Recruitment

The MWG [the Military Working Group that endorsed the enactment of the ban in 1993] found open homosexuality would reduce the propensity of many eligible young Americans to enlist due to parental concerns, peer pressure and a tarnished military image. Today, any reduction in propensity due to similar concerns would make recruiting even more challenging because due to other disqualifying criteria only three in ten American youth, ages 17–24, are eligible to serve.

Robert Maginnis,
"Gay Review & Combat Effectiveness,"
Human Events, *March 4, 2010.*

Driving Service Personnel Out of the Ranks

The authors acknowledge that 67 percent of all Marines, more than 60 percent of special-operations personnel, and 57 percent of soldiers in Army combat units believe changing the law would hurt military efficiency, unit cohesion, readiness, and retention. Overall, 35 percent of service members deployed overseas said that changing the law in current circumstances would have a negative impact on combat effectiveness. And, perhaps most telling, nearly one-third of all those who are now part of the best educated, best trained, and most combat-experienced military in history will consider "getting out" rather than serve side by side with openly homosexual men or lesbians.

Secretary Gates, Chairman Mullen, and other proponents of changing the law have concluded that "limited and isolated disruption to unit cohesion and retention" is "an acceptable risk"—even in the midst of a long and bloody war. They claim that any problems arising from repealing the ban will somehow be ameliorated by "careful planning, training and good leadership." What they cannot do is explain how the possibility of losing even 20 percent of today's active-duty military—more than 250,000 troops—could be anything but an *un*acceptable risk.

In nine years of covering every theater of this global war for Fox News and in writing *American Heroes in Special Operations*, I have never met a single senior non-commissioned officer in any service who said to me anything like: "We need some homosexuals and lesbians out here to help us accomplish our mission." What they do worry about is the prospect that thousands of our finest, most effective non-commissioned officers will leave the service at the end of their current enlistment and there won't be anyone around to train the next batch of replacements—assuming they can be recruited.

Disrespecting U.S. Troops in the Field

The report dismisses as a "short-term problem" the overwhelming moral and religious opposition expressed by military chaplains of every denomination. The SecDef's [secretary of defense's] "implementation plan" insists that "misperceptions" and "stereotypes" about living in close quarters with "openly gay service members" will be overcome by "revised standards of conduct" and "new regulations." Yet he also wants to "legalize consensual sodomy," prohibit "separate berthing, billeting or bathroom facilities based on sexual orientation," and deny honorable discharges to those who have a conscientious objection to living with a homosexual. Try explaining all that to the God-fearing, church-going parents of a 17-year-old prospective recruit.

None of this has to happen. And it won't—if the U.S. Senate simply refuses to repeal Section 654, Title X, USC. But that means at least 41 senators have to have enough courage not to dismantle the U.S. armed forces. [Editor's note: The ban on gays and lesbians serving openly in the military was overturned by Congress in September 2011.]

Our all-volunteer military, particularly the Marines, Army combat arms, and special-operations forces—and their families at home—are making extraordinary sacrifices to protect us from an implacable enemy. The young Americans I see on the battlefields of Mesopotamia and in the shadow of the Hindu Kush are warriors in the crucible of mortal combat. They deserve better than to be treated like lab rats in Mr. Obama's radical social experiment.

> *"In combat there are no excuses: your weapon kills or it jams; a buddy's got your back or he doesn't, no matter if you object to his personal habits."*

Tolerating Open Homosexuality in the Military Would Not Hurt Unit Effectiveness

David Wood

In the following viewpoint, military correspondent David Wood reports that the issue of homosexuals serving openly in the armed forces is not a significant threat to unit performance. As Wood argues, the issue is divided chiefly along generational lines, with older service personnel and politicians more concerned about repealing the ban on homosexuals than the younger frontline troops are concerned. As Wood asserts, young people have grown up in an era when tolerance and acceptance of homosexuality is commonly emphasized in school and in the media. In addition to this fact, Wood maintains that soldiers judge their comrades by bravery and competence, not by sexual orientation. David Wood has been a correspondent for Time *and other major publications, including* Politics Daily, *an online news source.*

David Wood, "Arguing About Gays in the Military: It's So Over," Politics Daily, February 3, 2010. www.politicsdaily.com.

As you read, consider the following questions:

1. As Wood reports, what did author Randy Shilts conclude in his *Conduct Unbecoming* about the impact of homosexuals serving in the military?

2. In what branch of the service does Wood believe the most prejudice against gays persists?

3. According to Wood, why did Senator John McCain believe the time was not right in 2010 to repeal the ban on homosexuals serving openly in the military?

Within the boisterous, hard-living ranks of enlisted soldiers and Marines, where I spend most of my reporting time, it's been 16 years since I heard anyone argue about whether the military should allow homosexuals to serve openly. And that was only because I asked. I was penned up with several hundred Marines on the amphibious assault ship *USS Barnstable County*, coming home from fighting in Somalia, and because I knew that back home in Washington, "Don't Ask, Don't Tell" [the policy that bans homosexuals from serving openly in the military] had become a big issue.

As we stood smoking and talking on the ship's pitching fantail, it was clear that many Marines considered gay sex disgusting and, some held, immoral. But they all identified a very clear bottom line: gay or straight, you are accepted if you can perform.

"We never ask anybody to join. You wanna be part of this outfit, you gotta meet the standards," one Marine said. "If you're a woman or a gay or a Martian, you gotta meet the standards. Otherwise go do something else."

Bravery and Competence Trump Concerns About Sexual Orientation

Infantrymen like these are a tough crowd. In their normal circumstances of stress and peril, they rely on physical touch for comfort and on the love and commitment of their comrades for safety. In combat there are no excuses: your weapon kills or it jams; a buddy's got your back or he doesn't, no matter if you object to his personal habits.

Warriors have always known this. In *Conduct Unbecoming: Gays & Lesbians in the U.S. Military*, an authoritative examination of gays in uniform, author Randy Shilts documented how homosexuality was always more of an issue in the peacetime military than when a fighting force was in the field. This makes sense to me—war has a way of concentrating the mind on what's important. In combat, competence, bravery, and common sense tend to trump partisan politics. And in the midst of two lengthy wars, this lesson seems to have been adopted by the nation these warriors are trying to protect: Some 70 percent of Americans now favor allowing gays and lesbians to serve openly in the armed forces.

And such attitudes now cut across all kinds of ideological lines. In November 2004, while Americans were re-electing George W. Bush to a second term, only 46 percent of his conservative base supported gays in the military. By May 2009, when a new commander in chief was just getting his sea legs, that number had risen to 58 percent, according to a Gallup poll.

Today's Soldiers Have More Tolerant Attitudes About Sexual Orientation

I believe that there has also been a sharp change in how the uniforms look at the issue. Today's military men and women— half of them under the age of 25—have grown up in a different environment, one of increasing acceptance of gays and lesbians. Many high schools have gay and lesbian organizations; "coming out" has ceased to be a curiosity; and much of the remnants of homophobia have simply evaporated with the passage of time. National surveys confirm these trends. In Washington, this issue is often filtered through a Republican-Democrat prism, but when it comes to gay rights, age is a stronger predictor than ideology. One of the sharpest demographic divisions pollsters have ever seen on a public policy issue occurs around gay marriage. Two-thirds of Americans over the age of 65 are opposed to gay marriage, while the "Millennial Generation"—those under 30 years of age—favor it . . . , says Gallup.

Now those kids are swarming into the military, bringing their attitudes with them.

Just last week [in January 2010], when I was living with 82nd Airborne Division troopers in Haiti, several soldiers mentioned in the course of conversation that they have friends who happen to be gay, including some in the military. (About 66,000 gays and lesbians currently serve in uniform, estimates Sen. Carl Levin, chairman of the Senate Armed Services Committee.)

I am sure there are exceptions. But in the 82nd Airborne and other units I've lived with, in Iraq and Afghanistan and elsewhere, it has become clear that gays and lesbians not only serve, but that their sexual orientation is unremarkable. The contrast of that attitude with older generations came into sharp focus Tuesday [February 2, 2010] when Republican Sen. John McCain, arguing against repeal of the "Don't Ask, Don't Tell" law, brandished a letter signed by "over one thousand retired general and flag officers" united against allowing gays and lesbians to serve openly. Indeed, opposition to gays and lesbians serving in the military seems to come mostly from those who are no longer serving in the military, or from those who never have. And the sentiment against gays has always seemed strongest in the U.S. Navy, perhaps because of the close quarters at sea—and perhaps because its culture can be hidebound.

Preparing for a Change

McCain, who most definitely served (and who served in the Navy), spoke at a hearing of the Senate Armed Services Committee called to weigh the implications of President [Barack]

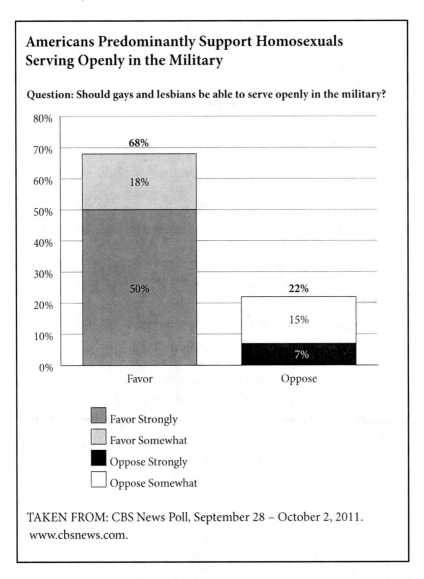

Americans Predominantly Support Homosexuals Serving Openly in the Military

Question: Should gays and lesbians be able to serve openly in the military?

TAKEN FROM: CBS News Poll, September 28 – October 2, 2011. www.cbsnews.com.

Obama's promise during his State of the Union speech Jan. 27 to work with Congress to repeal the 1993 law that says homosexuals can serve only if they do not reveal their sexual orientation.

Testifying Tuesday, Defense Secretary Robert Gates left unclear whether he personally believes "Don't Ask, Don't Tell" should be repealed. But he said he "fully supports" the president's decision. "The question before us is not whether the military prepares to make this change, but how we best prepare for it," Gates said. "We have received our orders from the commander in chief and we are moving out accordingly."

The argument for changing the law, advocates say, is one of both efficiency—some military people with critical skills such as Arabic translators have been discharged for being gay—and integrity. As Adm. Mike Mullen, chairman of the Joint Chiefs of Staff, said Tuesday, "Speaking for myself, allowing gays and lesbians to serve openly would be the right thing to do. . . . I cannot help being troubled by the fact that we force young men and women to lie about who they are in order to defend their fellow citizens."

Many gays and lesbians "serve admirably" in the military, McCain agreed, "and I honor their sacrifice and I honor them." He said the law has worked "successfully" for two decades, maintaining "good order and unit cohesion." He said current law "is well understood and predominantly supported by our fighting men and women." With two wars under way and the military under enormous stress, McCain said, this is no time to impose "substantial and controversial change" in the military's social order. Mullen countered: "I believe the brave young men and women of our military can and would accommodate" the repeal of the law and the open presence of gays and lesbians.

Doing away with the ban, as Obama has proposed, sounds easy enough—but it would hardly be the last step in the process and would plunge military leaders (and Congress) deep into some of the most divisive social issues of the day.

For instance, should single-sex military couples be given access to military housing for married couples? Should the partner of a lesbian officer receive the same health benefits as a legal spouse? Would that depend on whether they lived on a military base in a state that recognizes same-sex marriage?

Small wonder that Defense Secretary Gates, preparing to implement a change in the law, is giving a new high-level commission a full year to figure out how to do it.

[Editor's note: The ban on gays and lesbians serving openly in the military was overturned by Congress in September 2011.]

"The left-leaning [Supreme] Court even agreed that [the Boy Scouts of America] do have a right to ban gays, as they also do atheists and agnostics, under their 'constitutional right of freedom of association and free speech under the First Amendment.'"

The Boy Scouts of America Has a Right to Exclude Homosexuals

Lew Waters

In the viewpoint that follows, Lew Waters, a Vietnam War veteran, argues that the Boy Scouts of America is a valuable and venerable institution that teaches young people to honor and respect their country. However, Waters laments the fact that the Boy Scouts is just another victim of leftists who are intent on destroying any organization that teaches reverence for God and country. The current assault aims at forcing the Boy Scouts to accept homosexuals, Waters states. He believes that the Boy Scouts has a right to exclude because it is a private organization, an opinion so far shared by the courts. Waters contends that attacks on such important American institutions suggest that America is continuing its moral slide toward socialism.

Lew Waters, "What Good Are the Boy Scouts?," Right in a Left World, October 21, 2007. http://rightinaleftworld.blogspot.com.

159

As you read, consider the following questions:

1. Where does Waters think children will learn about homosexual lifestyles even if it is kept out of the Boy Scouts?

2. Why did the Boy Scouts lose its lease to San Diego's Balboa Park, according to Waters?

3. What public figure does Waters claim may not have learned to honor his country despite his Boy Scouts training?

Most everyone has heard of the Boy Scouts of America. At one time, they were well respected and looked upon as a good organization, preparing boys to be men, teaching patriotism, discipline, love of God and country and such.

When I was a Boy Scout we learned many skills. Camping, fire building, cooking, swimming, first aid and even basic survival, to an extent. We were taught to be TRUSTWORTHY, LOYAL, HELPFUL, FRIENDLY, COURTEOUS, KIND, OBEDIENT, CHEERFUL, THRIFTY, BRAVE, CLEAN and REVERENT. We lived by the Scout motto, Be Prepared. We were taught respect of our flag as well as proper flag etiquette.

Many of those skills helped me make it through my time in Vietnam and gave me a foundation for life that has seen me through many downturns, encouraging me to just pick myself back up and keep going.

You might even call the Boy Scouts of America the original green group, as our common practice when camping was to leave the land cleaner than we found it. We were taught to respect nature and not to litter.

Another American Institution Under Attack

Sadly, for quite a few years now, the organization has become the target of leftists who see it as a danger to their leftist ideology and it must be ridiculed, infiltrated and eventually destroyed. Anything that teaches a deep reverence to God and to America spells trouble to the socialist-leaning left.

To disrupt and eventually destroy the organization, somewhere along the line they became a target of the leftist ACLU [American Civil Liberties Union] because they did not accept gays as scouts or adult scout leaders. For years, the battle has been ongoing to either disband the organization or force them to accept gays, against the wishes of the scouts and their parents.

It isn't like these young men will be denied any information on gay lifestyle as we all know that public schools cram it down our kids' throats every chance they get.

Taken before the Supreme Court of the United States, the left-leaning court even agreed that they do have a right to ban gays, as they also do atheists and agnostics, under their "constitutional right of freedom of association and free speech under the First Amendment." By a 5-4 vote in June of 2000, the court overturned a lower court ruling and upheld the Scouts' right to determine by their moral code who can and cannot belong.

Of course that didn't set well with leftists, even though other lower courts for years upheld their right to select who they felt was best to be leading impressionable young boys. So the attacks continued.

Undermining Public Service

Look to San Diego's Balboa Park. 16 acres leased to the Boy Scouts for $1 a year and that they maintained, rebuilt and by fund-raising and volunteer work, had a state-of-the-art swimming pool and 600-seat outdoor amphitheater built. The Boy Scouts have faithfully maintained the grounds, and the park has been available to all citizens, not just the Boy Scouts.

We can thank the ACLU now for stepping in and protecting citizens from this organization as they sued on behalf of a lesbian couple and an agnostic couple. U.S. District Judge Napoleon Jones Jr. ruled the Boy Scouts as a religion and therefore their lease of the park was unconstitutional under the separation of church and state canard. City Councilwoman Toni Atkins, herself a lesbian, commented, "Now it's up to the Boy Scouts to respond and stop discriminating."

In the meantime, the park must be maintained by the city at millions of dollars of expense, where the Boy Scouts were doing it for free.

It doesn't stop there.

For as long as I can recall, the Scouts hold a national jamboree every four years, with federal support from the Department of Defense in the form of "non-religious supplies and services." They have been supportive in this manner for 60 years. Yet, in 1999 the ACLU filed suit again over "separation of church and state." They lost that one.

Undeterred, leftists still assault the Boy Scouts every chance they can get. In Philadelphia, Pennsylvania, an openly gay activist city solicitor has raised the Scouts rent for their offices in a landmark Philadelphia building by a whopping $199,999! To return to their long-held $1-a-year rent, all they need to do is allow gays to be adult leaders of young boys and members.

After the loud outcry these past few years over gay priests abusing young boys for decades, one would think the Boy Scouts would receive recognition for protecting youthful members. As can be seen above, such is not the case as gay activists and the ACLU have decided this organization must either accept gays or die.

Teaching Values That Seem to Be Lacking Today

Since their inception in 1910, the Boy Scouts of America have prepared many famous men for adulthood and even public service. While they have produced American heroes, industrial giants, athletes, veterans and politicians, a few have slipped through without learning the honor our country seems to be lacking today.

One such would be senator and presidential candidate [in 2007] Barack Obama. A former classmate claimed that he and Obama were in the Boy Scouts together while in school in Indonesia. Although not the Boy Scouts of America, international scouting teaches much the same thing in values, respect and honor.

Obama has come out refusing to wear an American flag lapel pin. More recently he was spotted at a barbecue for [US senator from Iowa] Tom Harkin standing [with his hands folded at his waist instead of over his heart] during the playing of our National Anthem.

He sure didn't pick up such disrespect from the Boy Scouts of America.

Our country is in a slide downward as the values and respect we were taught as youths are under fire and being discarded left and right. Conservative values are scoffed at and ridiculed, even though America was founded on them and stood strong for decades by them. The Boy Scouts of America have been teaching young boys for nearly a century,

On my honor I will do my best

To do my duty to God and my country

And to obey the Scout Law;

To help other people at all times;

To keep myself physically strong,

Mentally awake, and morally straight.

We need the Boy Scouts, leave them alone!

> "Protesters said they were looking for a conversation and not a confrontation over the organization's policy barring homosexuals from its ranks."

Group Protests Scout's Gay Policy

Angela K. Brown

In the following viewpoint, Angela K. Brown discusses the Boy Scouts of America's antigay stance and the opposition the organization faces because of its beliefs. Brown introduces Corey Brunson, a mother of a four-year-old boy who wants her son to join the organization but only if it changes its rules on admitting homosexuals. Brunson believes the group is being discriminatory and judgmental. Brown maintains that although the heads of the organization believe admitting homosexuals into the group would run counter to the organization's oath to be "morally straight," the public is protesting this rule. Angela K. Brown is a contributor and writer for the Associated Press.

As you read, consider the following questions:

1. Who is Corey Brunson, as stated in the viewpoint?

2. According to the viewpoint, is the Boy Scouts budging from its position on homosexuality?

3. What does Gregg Shields say homosexuality runs counter to within the context of the organization?

Irving, Texas (AP)—Corey Brunson wants her 4-year-old son to join the Boy Scouts in a few years—but only if the organization alters its antigay stance.

"This judgmental attitude and discrimination is going on, and I don't think this is right," she said. "I reject the notion that this is a private organization. It couldn't survive without public support."

Brunson joined about a dozen marchers Monday who delivered a 55,000-signature petition to the Boy Scouts of America headquarters in Irving, near Dallas. Similar rallies were planned in front of Boy Scouts offices in 36 cities in 21 states.

Protesters said they were looking for a conversation and not a confrontation over the organization's policy barring homosexuals from its ranks.

"We're disappointed," Dave Rice, a former scout leader who marched in Irving. "We don't like confrontation. We like to sit down, shake hands and discuss a solution that's mutually beneficial."

Despite the public pressure, the Boys Scouts weren't budging from their position on gays.

Gregg Shields, spokesman for the National Council of the Boy Scouts of America, said homosexuality runs counter to the oath requiring scouts to be "morally straight."

"We recognize the rights of all people to hold opinions different than ours," he said. "We stress that we are a private organization and that no one is forced to be a Boy Scout. People who share our values and beliefs are welcome to join."

In June, the Supreme Court agreed, ruling 5-4 that the group was allowed to bar homosexuals.

Scouting for All, a nonprofit organization, helped organize and coordinate the nationwide protests. Its founder, Steven Cozza, 15, of Petaluma, Calif., said he started the group several years ago after his father was removed as a scout leader for supporting gay rights.

"Scoutmasters are people to look up to. What's wrong with being influenced by a gay man? Someone's sexuality has nothing to do with his character or personality," Cozza said.

Cozza, who said neither he nor his father is gay, left the Boy Scouts about six months ago after becoming an Eagle Scout.

Not all support Cozza's efforts.

Nick Henderson, a Boy Scout leader in Dallas, said he thinks homosexuality is a sin and supports the scouting policy.

"We don't want them in a position of leadership," he said. "We're not against gay people; just their lifestyle. Would they be a bad influence on a scout troop? Absolutely."

In San Leandro, Calif., about 20 people walked outside the Boy Scouts' San Francisco Bay Area office, chanting and toting signs saying "Blatant Bigots" and "True leaders teach love and tolerance, not hate and bigotry."

"I'm not here to be disrespectful to the Boy Scouts of America. But we can't be silent," said Jan Tyler, a Bay Area Cub Scout leader. "Gays and lesbians are in every niche in our society, and to exclude them based on sexual orientation is ludicrous."

| *"Most gay priests are not molesters, but most of the molesters have been gay."*

The Sexual Abuse Problems of the Catholic Church Are Rooted in Homosexuality

Bill Donohue

The Catholic Church has struggled to match its doctrine that defines homosexuality as a "moral evil" with the acknowledged fact that a minority of clergy are gay. The church has attempted to deal with the issue by emphasizing the need for chastity among the priesthood. In the late twentieth and early twenty-first centuries, several scandals arose from various dioceses in which Catholic priests were accused of sexually abusing young boys. In the following viewpoint, Bill Donohue claims that in almost every instance, the abuser was either gay or had previous homosexual relationships. For this reason, and because many of the male victims were postpubescent, Donohue argues that the problem is one of homosexuality, not pedophilia. Though he maintains that not all gay priests are abusers, Donohue insists that to hide the connection between homosexuality and the abuse is dishonest. Bill Donohue is the president of the Catholic League for Religious and Civil Rights, a church advocacy organization.

As you read, consider the following questions:

1. Why does Donohue stress that the link between homosexuality and the abuse in the church is a matter of correlation if not causation?

2. As the author states, what characteristics of nearly four hundred abuse victims did Roderick MacLeish uncover in his examination of the church scandals?

3. How does Donohue feel about policies that would seek to bar homosexuals from the priesthood?

Anthony Stevens-Arroyo [an American religious scholar] says I am wrong to challenge elite opinion on the subject of priestly sexual abuse. The conventional wisdom maintains there is a pedophilia crisis in the Catholic Church; I maintain it has been a homosexual crisis all along. The evidence is all on my side, though there is a reluctance to let the data drive the conclusion. But that is a function of politics, not scholarship.

A Well-Founded Link

[American sexologist] Alfred Kinsey was the first to identify a correlation between homosexuality and the sexual abuse of minors. In 1948, he found that 37 percent of all male homosexuals admitted to having sex with children under 17 years old. More recently, in organs such as the *Archives of Sexual Behavior*, the *Journal of Sex Research*, the *Journal of Sex and Marital Therapy* and *Pediatrics*, it has been established that homosexuals are disproportionately represented among child molesters.

Correlation is not causation; it is an association. So to say that there is a correlation between homosexual orientation and the sexual abuse of minors is not to say that being a homosexual makes one a molester. Indeed, as I have said many times, most gay priests are not molesters, but most of the molesters have been gay. In other words, although sexual orientation does not cause sexual abuse, the fact that there is a relationship between homosexuality and the sexual abuse of minors cannot be ignored in dealing with this problem.

Think of it this way. We know there is a correlation between being Irish and being an alcoholic, but that doesn't mean all Irishmen are, or will become, alcoholics. But it does mean they have a special problem in this area. Does this now make me anti-Irish?

National Review Board Findings

When the National Review Board [of the United States Conference of Catholic Bishops] released its findings in 2004 regarding priestly sexual abuse, Robert S. Bennett, the noted attorney who headed the study, said, "There are no doubt many outstanding priests of a homosexual orientation who live chaste, celibate lives, but any evaluation of the causes and context of the current crisis must be cognizant of the fact that more than 80 percent of the abuse at issue was of a homosexual nature." Were they wrong to draw this conclusion?

Furthermore, the National Review Board explicitly said that "we must call attention to the homosexual behavior that characterized the vast majority of the cases of abuse observed in recent decades." So what's stopping others from drawing this conclusion?

One of those who served on the National Review Board, Dr. Paul McHugh, is a former psychiatrist-in-chief at Johns Hopkins [University School of Medicine]. He is on record saying, "This behavior was homosexual predation on American Catholic youth, yet it's not being discussed." And we know why: There are penalties for telling the truth.

Roderick MacLeish Jr. was the Boston lawyer who pressed the case against the Archdiocese of Boston; he examined all the files on this subject. As reported by Michael Paulson in the *Boston Globe*, MacLeish concluded that "90 percent of the nearly 400 sexual abuse victims he has represented are boys, and three-quarters of them are postpubescent." Once again, the issue is homosexuality, not pedophilia.

Every Accused Priest Had Previous Homosexual Adult Encounters

Dr. Richard Fitzgibbons is a psychiatrist who has spent years treating sexually abusive priests. "Many psychologists and psychiatrists have shown that there is no link between celibacy and pedophilia," he said earlier this year [2010]. Instead, they have found a "relationship between homosexuality and pedophilia." So are all of these psychologists and psychiatrists wrong?

In fact, Fitzgibbons says, "every priest whom I treated who was involved with children sexually had previously been involved in adult homosexual relationships." Notice he didn't say "some" priests.

Three months ago, the *New York Times* ran a story on Leslie Lothstein, another psychologist who has treated abusive priests. He concluded that "only a small minority were true pedophiles." Is he wrong, too?

The *Boston Globe*, which won a Pulitzer Prize for disclosing the scandal, said of the John Jay [College of Criminal Justice] study, which was released at the same time, that "more than three-quarters of the victims were postpubescent, meaning the abuse did not meet the clinical definition of pedophilia." So if the definitive study, which covered the years 1950–2002, concludes that pedophilia was never the issue, then why does everyone from Tony Stevens-Arroyo to the *New York Times* insist that there is a "pedophilia crisis" in the Catholic Church?

I have said before, and I will say it again, that I am opposed to any policy that unequivocally bars homosexual men from the priesthood. But, knowing the data, it would be foolish not to screen more closely for homosexually active men entering the priesthood. That is exactly what the Vatican is doing.

In the end, I am not going to stop telling the truth about the link between homosexuality and the sexual abuse of minors. The evidence is overwhelming, and only political considerations get in the way of being honest about it.

> *"Certainly there were homosexually oriented priests who were abusers, just as there were heterosexually oriented abusers.... But, as the new [John Jay] study shows, the vast majority of homosexual priests (and heterosexual priests) never abused anyone."*

Gay Priests Should Not Be Scapegoats for the Sexual Abuse Problems in the Catholic Church

James Martin

In the wake of child sexual abuse scandals that arose in the Catholic Church in the late twentieth and early twenty-first centuries, both the Catholic leadership and parishioners had to face the alarming revelation that members of the priesthood had been using their positions to molest young boys. Some commentators both within and outside the church argued that the abuse stemmed from the homosexual desires of the accused priests. In the following viewpoint, James Martin claims that this assumption is unfounded. Citing legal reviews of the scandals, psycho-

James Martin, "John Jay Report: On Not Blaming Homosexual Priests," *America Magazine*, May 17, 2011. Copyright © 2011 by America Magazine. All rights reserved. Reproduced by permission.

logical studies, and his own experience with gay priests, Martin insists that homosexuality is not linked to child sexual abuse. Instead, Martin notes that the rise in the number of gay priests in recent decades corresponds to a decline in reported abuses and that many gay priests—like heterosexual priests—are dutiful, celibate servants of God. Martin believes that to scapegoat gay priests will only increase fears and denigrate the works of those loyal men who have devoted their lives to their parishes. James Martin is a Jesuit priest and the culture editor of America, *a national Catholic weekly.*

As you read, consider the following questions:

1. According to Martin, psychologists commonly link pedophilia to what causes?

2. Why does Martin believe the stereotype that gay priests are pedophiles persists in the public and the church?

3. As the author explains, how did various church officials react to the Vatican's 2004 letter that concluded "men with 'deep-seated homosexual tendencies' should not be admitted to the priesthood"?

The new John Jay report[1] on the "causes and contexts" of the sexual abuse crisis in the Catholic Church includes a finding that will probably surprise many observers. As David Gibson states in a piece on Religion News Service:

> [T]he researchers found no statistical evidence that gay priests were more likely than straight priests to abuse minors—a finding that undermines a favorite talking point of many conservative Catholics. The disproportionate number of adolescent male victims was about opportunity, not preference or pathology, the report states.

1. A report originally posted in 2004 by the John Jay College of Criminal Justice detailed the institution's investigation of sexual abuse allegations in the Catholic Church. The college issued a new report on the allegations in 2011.

What's more, researchers note that the rise in the number of gay priests from the late 1970s onward actually corresponded with "a decreased incidence of abuse—not an increased incidence of abuse."

How is this possible, particularly given the widespread stereotype of the abusive or predatory homosexual priest? How else to explain so many male victims of abuse?

Studies Refute the Supposed Link Between Homosexuality and Pedophilia

First of all, nearly every reputable psychologist and psychiatrist, not to mention almost every scholarly study, decisively rejects the conflation of homosexuality with pedophilia, as well as any cause-and-effect relationship. The studies are almost too numerous to mention. Pedophilia, say experts, is often more a question of a stunted (or arrested) sexuality, more a question of power, and more a question of proximity (among other complicated psychological and social factors). The new John Jay College of Criminal Justice study, called "The Causes and Context of Sexual Abuse of Minors by Catholic Priests in the United States, 1950–2010," points to, among other reasons: emotionally immature and psychologically maladjusted men entering seminaries; the difficulty of dealing with cultural upheaval in which priests found themselves in the 1960s and 1970s; as well as, again, the issue of proximity—young men and boys were abused because priests were more likely to be working with them, rather than with young women and girls. But simply put, being a homosexual priest does not make one an abusive priest.

Indeed, the U.S. Conference of Catholic Bishops commissioned another extensive independent study in the wake of the American abuse crisis in 2002, also undertaken by John Jay College. In 2009, Margaret Smith, a researcher from John Jay, reported to the bishops, "What we are suggesting is that the idea of sexual identity be separated from the problem of sexual abuse. At this point, we do not find a connection between homosexual identity and the increased likelihood of subsequent abuse from the data that we have right now."

Second, there is a stronger argument against the frequent conflation of homosexuality and pedophilia: the lived experience of emotionally mature and psychologically healthy gay men (and women) who have never, ever abused a child; are not tempted to do so; are not attracted to children at all; and would, in short, never think of doing so. Being gay does not make one a pedophile.

This insight is, I believe, known by thoughtful bishops, experienced church leaders and seasoned Vatican officials. That is one reason why last year [in 2010] the Rev. Marcus Stock, the general secretary of the Catholic Bishops' Conference of England and Wales, released a statement saying, "To the best of my knowledge, there is no empirical data which concludes that sexual orientation is connected to child sexual abuse. The consensus among researchers is that the sexual abuse of children is not a question of sexual 'orientation', whether heterosexual or homosexual, but of a disordered attraction or 'fixation.'"

Uncovering the Origins of a Harmful Stereotype

But despite the findings of the new John Jay report, and the warnings of psychology professionals against equating pedophilia and abuse, some both inside and outside the church may still find this new study difficult to accept. If these findings were true, they may ask, why would so many victims be not just young boys but adolescent males? Once again, researchers have always suggested that this has more to do with a welter of reasons, including proximity: Many priests were in the past responsible for the care of boys. In schools and parish settings, Catholic sisters cared for girls; priests for boys.

Certainly there were homosexually oriented priests who were abusers, just as there were heterosexually oriented abusers. (That much should be clear to anyone who has followed this terrible saga since 2002.) But, as the new study shows, the vast majority of homosexual priests (and heterosexual priests) never abused anyone. In fact, the increased numbers of homosexual priests coincided with a *decrease* in abuse cases. So where does the stereotype of the abusive homosexual priest come from? Here is where the situation grows more complex.

One of the main reasons that many persist in thinking that homosexuality is the root cause of the abuse crisis, and that homosexual priests are mainly pedophiles, is because there are almost no "public" models of healthy, mature, loving celibate homosexual priests to rebut that stereotype. An *America* magazine article published in 2000 looked at some of the reasons why.

There are in the Catholic priesthood, and there have always been, celibate homosexual priests and chaste homosexual members of religious orders. How do I know this? Because, like most priests, I have known a few of them. They are emotionally mature, psychologically healthy, genuinely loving, and beloved by those with whom they minister; they work hard on behalf of the "People of God," and they have never abused a single child. Many of these men are among the holiest people I've ever known. I consider a few of them saints. And let me repeat, so as to be clear: They are *celibate*. Or, in religious orders, they are *chaste*. (As an aside, using the word "gay priest" sets off alarm bells in some corners of the church, where "gay" is assumed to mean sexually active.)

Why Gay Priests May Hide Their Sexual Orientation

Some of these men are public about their orientations only with close friends, their confessors or their spiritual directors. The reasons for nondisclosure are easy to identify, even if they are not always easy for the general public to understand.

Some Conclusions Drawn by the John Jay Report

• Less than 5 percent of the priests with allegations of abuse exhibited behavior consistent with a diagnosis of pedophilia (a psychiatric disorder that is characterized by recurrent fantasies, urges, and behaviors about *prepubescent* children). Thus, it is inaccurate to refer to abusers as "pedophile priests."

• Sexual behavior in violation of the commitment to celibacy was reported by 80 percent of the priests who participated in residential psychological treatment, but most sexual behavior was with adults.

• Priests who had same-sex sexual experiences either before seminary or in seminary were more likely to have sexual behavior after ordination, but this behavior was most likely with adults. These men were not significantly more likely to abuse minors.

• Priests who were sexually abused as minors themselves were more likely to abuse minors than those without a history of abuse.

"The Causes and Context of Sexual Abuse of Minors by Catholic Priests in the United States, 1950–2010," John Jay College of Criminal Justice, May 2011.

First, these priests may be fearful of how their parishioners would react, especially if they are living in a parish where homophobia abounds. Second, they might feel, not without reason, that a public declaration might place more emphasis on the priest than on his ministry and, likewise, serve as a distraction and even cause a serious division within the parish. Third, they might be fearful of reprisals or punishments by some less-than-understanding bishops or religious superiors.

Fourth, they may be unable or unwilling to do so for a variety of personal reasons. (For example, they may be of a generation where talk of sexuality simply wasn't done, or they may still be deeply embarrassed by their orientation, despite their celibacy and chastity.) And, in the wake of the abuse crisis, when some commentators linked homosexuality with pedophilia, some of their fears intensified. Finally, some priests may be explicitly forbidden by their bishops or religious superiors, fearful of publicity, from speaking about their orientation publicly.

Reactions to the Scandal in the Church

Some of this came to a boil with the release of the Vatican's 2004 letter, completed after a lengthy Vatican "visitation" of the U.S. seminaries in the wake of the abuse crisis. The document, "Instruction Concerning the Criteria for the Discernment of Vocations with Regard to Persons with Homosexual Tendencies in View of Their Admission to the Seminary and to Holy Orders," stated that men with "deep-seated homosexual tendencies" could not be admitted to the priesthood.

Since then, the document has been interpreted in various ways in diocesan seminaries and in formation programs in religious orders, at least according to officials with whom I've spoken with in the intervening years. Last year, a diocesan seminarian wrote to tell me that in his seminary there was a "don't tell your brothers" policy, while in other seminaries any admission of one's homosexuality can lead, as I am told, to expulsion. On the other hand, some bishops and superiors of religious orders, recognizing the historical contributions of celibate gay priests, have interpreted the document to mean that "deep-seated" means that one cannot live celibately; ergo, if a gay man feels an authentic call to the priesthood, is emotionally mature and can live a celibate lifestyle, he can be ordained. One of the most pastoral approaches comes from Timothy Dolan, archbishop of New York, who wisely said on the document's release that a man who is homosexual and feels a vocation to be a priest "shouldn't be discouraged." Other bishops and religious superiors—it is admittedly difficult to say how many—have adopted similar approaches.

Fears Remain

Still, the fear among many celibate homosexual clergy remains. Not long ago, an experienced priest with many years in parish ministry told me that the only way that things will change is when all the homosexual priests decide one Sunday to "come out" to their parishes. But that is highly unlikely: Besides the reasons stated above, the bonds that tie these men together are usually local, and mostly informal. Nonetheless, something of that nature could serve as a significant "teaching moment" for the entire church. On the other hand, many Catholic parishioners aren't ignorant of this fact: They are most likely aware that some of their priests are homosexual, and as long as they're celibate and loving and generous and prayerful, parishioners are accepting of them, and are usually grateful. The inspiring story of the Rev. Fred Daley, of Utica, New York, is one such example.

Most Catholics—including most bishops and archbishops—already know these things. The new John Jay report will only confirm their accepting approach to the celibate homosexual clergy with whom they have worked over the years. They know that homosexuality and pedophilia are not the same thing. (This may be why Pope Benedict XVI himself, en route to the United States for his visit in 2008, responded this way to a question about the abuse crisis: "I do not wish to talk about homosexuality, but about pedophilia, which is a different thing.") They also know that there are many celibate homosexual men in the priesthood and chaste men in religious orders who have never abused anyone and who, moreover, lead generous, dedicated, and even holy lives.

Periodical and Internet Sources Bibliography

The following articles have been selected to supplement the diverse views presented in this chapter.

Derek J. Burks	"Lesbian, Gay, and Bisexual Victimization in the Military: An Unintended Consequence of 'Don't Ask, Don't Tell'?," *American Psychologist*, October 2011.
Ann Coulter	"Liberals, Priests and Boy Scouts," *Human Events*, March 25, 2002.
Robert M. Hill	"Soldiers All," *Military Review*, November/December 2011.
Karl B. Johnson	"Goodbye to All That," *Time*, October 3, 2011.
Rebecca Jones	"The Boy Scouts and Discrimination: Be Prepared!," *Education Digest*, September 2001.
Peter Katel	"Future of the Catholic Church," *CQ Researcher*, January 19, 2007.
Lisa Neff	"Mormons on a Mission," *Advocate*, March 22, 2005.
Laurie Penny	"Proud to Say Nope to the Pope," *New Statesman*, September 17, 2010.
Michelangelo Signorile	"Rewriting History," *Advocate*, February 17, 2011.
Ari Ezra Waldman	"Commentary & Reply: Military Justice Is Alive and Well," *Parameters: US Army War College*, Spring 2011.
Cheryl Wetzstein	"Boy Scouts Will Not Allow Gays to Join," *Washington Times*, July 17, 2012.

For Further Discussion

Chapter 1

1. Dan Eden claims that scientific studies link homosexuality with early brain development. What evidence does he provide to support his argument? Why does Robert H. Knight refute this causative connection? What evidence does he contribute to the debate? Whose view do you find more convincing? What do you feel is at stake in being able to assert that homosexuality either is or is not inborn? Explain your answer.

2. *Catholic Insight* reports that some supporters of Marine General Peter Pace's comments affirm that the Bible condemns homosexuality as immoral, but Chris Ayers, a pastor of a church, believes selective readings of the Bible ignore greater lessons about compassion for all humanity. Why do you think these leaders and spokespeople can have such divergent views of Scripture? Explain your answer.

Chapter 2

1. Jason Frye claims that marriage has always been predominantly a civil institution and that same-sex marriage should be tolerated because it supports that institution. Vigen Guroian, on the other hand, insists that, for Christians, marriage is a holy union that reflects God's design in human procreation and therefore rejects homosexual couplings. Citing evidence from these and any other viewpoints, clearly explain which interpretation you favor, or offer an alternative to these two understandings of the marriage contract that might reconcile or make unnecessary some of the implied contentions.

2. After reading the four viewpoints in this chapter, explain why you think same-sex marriage is such a hotly contested issue. Why does it matter to each of these authors that same-sex marriage be endorsed, tolerated, or condemned in America? For example, Vigen Guroian asserts that same-sex marriage defies God's plan. What are some of the other issues that touch on the same-sex marriage debate or would be impacted by any resolution on same-sex marriage, as the authors explain?

3. Christopher M. Gacek argues that the Defense of Marriage Act (DOMA) is a vital law because it upholds traditional notions of marriage and preserves each state's right to maintain that tradition. What type of debate strategy does Gacek use to make his case? Do you find his argument convincing? Explain.

Chapter 3

1. Enumerate the reasons Jerome Hunt and Jeffrey Krehely give for allowing homosexual couples to adopt children. Then, list the reasons Gregory Rogers provides for restricting homosexual adoption. Explain what you think informs each of their views and decide which argument you find more convincing. Examine how you reached that decision and why you ultimately chose to favor one side over the other.

2. What kind of reasoning does Andrew Haines utilize in refuting the notion that homosexual adoption should be tolerated in the interest of providing more potential parents for children? Does his rejection of the "greater good" argument appear logically sound? Why or why not? Use quotes from his viewpoint and that of Kerry Hosking to explain your reasoning.

3. After reading the four viewpoints in this chapter, give your opinion on what rights, if any, homosexual individuals or same-sex couples should have in adopting children.

What authority should determine whether homosexuals can adopt? Are there instances in which adoption should be forbidden to homosexual individuals or same-sex couples? What do you feel society ultimately gains or loses by sanctioning homosexual adoption? Use opinions from the viewpoints to support your conclusions.

Chapter 4

1. Oliver North claims that allowing homosexual military personnel to openly express their sexual orientation might offend other service persons and lead to poor morale and perhaps the resignation of many combat troops. Does North have a strong argument? Should concerns over the cohesion of America's forces trump the personal motivations of homosexual soldiers who do not wish to hide their sexual identities? Reread David Wood's viewpoint as well and explain what you believe should be the rules regarding the accommodation of homosexuals in the military.

2. The viewpoints by Lew Waters and Angela K. Brown debate the right of private organizations—such as the Boy Scouts of America—to ban homosexuals from active membership. Using the arguments forwarded by Waters and Brown, explain what benefits or costs you perceive will arise from supporting such rights.

3. Bill Donohue contends that the scandals involving Catholic priests engaging in sexual relationships with boys in their care stem from the homosexual proclivities of those priests. James Martin, however, fears that attributing the inappropriate behavior to homosexuality would be unwise and dangerous. In Martin's opinion, not all gay priests are driven to molest boys and to scapegoat all gay priests for the inexcusable acts of a few would discredit the good works of those gay men who remain loyal servants of God and their congregations. After reading these two view-

points, what is your opinion on the matter? Neither Martin nor Donohue advocate barring gay men from the priesthood, but is Donohue correct in asserting that the church must screen more closely for homosexually active men who seek to be ordained, or would that lead to some unforeseen consequences? Explain.

Organizations to Contact

The editors have compiled the following list of organizations concerned with the issues debated in this book. The descriptions are derived from materials provided by the organizations. All have publications or information available for interested readers. The list was compiled on the date of publication of the present volume; the information provided here may change. Be aware that many organizations take several weeks or longer to respond to inquiries, so allow as much time as possible.

American Civil Liberties Union (ACLU)
125 Broad Street, 18th Floor, New York, NY   10004
(212) 549-2500
website: www.aclu.org

The American Civil Liberties Union (ACLU) seeks to preserve the rights of all Americans as guaranteed by the Constitution, with a particular focus on the rights of historically underrepresented groups, including people of color; women; lesbians, gay men, bisexuals, and transgender people; prisoners; and people with disabilities. The Lesbian, Gay, Bisexual, and Transgender (LGBT) Project offers programs dedicated to ensuring members of this community have the same opportunities to live happy, successful lives as other Americans. The ACLU's work on this issue can be divided into basic rights and liberties, parenting, relationships and marriage, youth and schools, and discrimination against transgender people. The ACLU website provides detailed information about the organization's campaigns, court cases, policy suggestions, and reports along with general information about national and state LGBT laws.

American Enterprise Institute for Public Policy Research (AEI)
1150 Seventeenth Street NW, Washington, DC   20036
(202) 862-5800 • fax: (202) 862-7177
website: www.aei.org

Since its founding in 1943, the American Enterprise Institute for Public Policy Research (AEI), a private, nonpartisan think tank, has worked to promote the principles of liberty, individual opportunity, and free enterprise by conducting research and then educating the public and policy makers about its findings. Areas of focus include economics, foreign and defense policy, politics and public opinion, education, health, energy and the environment, and society and culture. Under the society and culture umbrella, AEI scholars have participated in the debate concerning the rights of homosexual individuals in the United States, with most attention going to the issue of gay marriage. In publications such as "Stop Courts from Imposing Gay Marriage" and "Redefining Marriage Away," commentators have opposed altering the legal definition of marriage to include same-sex couples; however, "Go-Slow Approach on Gay Amendment a Departure in House" cautions against passing a constitutional amendment to ban gay marriage. Additional commentary and articles providing statistics about public opinion on this issue can be found on the AEI website.

Cato Institute

1000 Massachusetts Avenue NW
Washington, DC   20001-5403
(202) 842-0200 • fax: (202) 842-2400
website: www.cato.org

The Cato Institute, a libertarian public policy organization, works to advance the ideals of individual liberty, limited governments, free markets, and peace. Through its research, conferences, and publications, the organization promotes policy that aligns with these basic principles. As such, Cato scholars have generally supported efforts to legalize gay marriage, viewing it as a civil liberties issue. Articles such as "The Moral and Constitutional Case for a Right to Gay Marriage" and multimedia files such as "The Constitutional Case for Marriage Equality" further explore this view. These materials along with others can be accessed on Cato's website.

Concerned Women for America (CWA)
1015 Fifteenth Street NW, Suite 1100, Washington, DC 20005
(202) 488-7000 • fax: (202) 488-0806
e-mail: mail@cwfa.org
website: www.cwfa.org

Concerned Women for America (CWA) is a public policy women's organization that advocates for the integration of biblical principles into public policy at the local, state, and national levels. The organization works within six main areas— the family, the sanctity of human life, religious education, pornography, and national sovereignty—and opposes gay marriage and adoption, seeing them as undermining traditional family values. Reports on these topics, such as "'Sexual Orientation' and American Culture," can be found on CWA's website.

Focus on the Family
8605 Explorer Drive, Colorado Springs, CO 80920
800-232-6459
e-mail: help@FocusontheFamily.com
website: www.focusonthefamily.com

Focus on the Family is a Christian ministry that offers assistance and resources to couples around the world to aid them in crafting marriages that are true to God's plan and to parents so they can instill biblical morals and values in their children. In accordance with these beliefs, the organization opposes gay marriage and adoption by gay parents, maintaining that marriage is between a man and a woman as stated in the Bible and asserting that to develop properly, children must be raised by a mother and father. Articles and videos expanding on this view can be read or watched on the Focus on the Family website.

Freedom to Marry
155 W. Nineteenth Street, 2nd Floor, New York, NY 10011
(212) 851-8418 • fax: (646) 375-2069
website: www.freedomtomarry.org

Freedom to Marry is a national campaign with the goal of increasing the number of states allowing same-sex couples to legally marry and ending federal discrimination—in the form of the Defense of Marriage Act—against gay marriage. The campaign website provides detailed information about action being taken to achieve organizational goals along with facts about state and federal legislation governing marriage. The campaign's blog provides timely information concerning campaign achievements and action.

Gay and Lesbian Alliance Against Defamation (GLAAD)
5455 Wilshire Boulevard, #1500, Los Angeles, CA   90036
(323) 933-2240 • fax: (323) 933-2241
website: www.glaad.org

The Gay and Lesbian Alliance Against Defamation (GLAAD) has worked for more than twenty-five years to highlight the stories of lesbian, gay, bisexual, and transgender (LGBT) people in the news, entertainment industry, and social media with the intent of enacting social change. The organization describes its role as that of a storyteller of the LGBT community, a watchdog who ensures the accuracy of media LGBT portrayals, and an advocate for LGBT rights. Information about the range of GLAAD media programs in addition to publications aimed at advancing LGBT rights can be found on the organization's website.

Heritage Foundation
214 Massachusetts Avenue NE, Washington, DC   20002-4999
(202) 546-4400
e-mail: info@heritage.org
website: www.heritage.org

The Heritage Foundation is a conservative research organization that promotes public policy espousing the values of free enterprise, limited government, individual freedom, traditional American values, and a strong national defense. The organization sees traditional marriage as the center of a strong country and opposes the legalization of same-sex marriage.

The foundation's website provides commentary on the issue in the form of research, congressional testimony, and articles, including "Same-Sex Marriage and Threats to Religious Freedom: How Nondiscrimination Laws Factor In" and "The Defense of Marriage Act: A Measure for Children and Families."

Human Rights Campaign (HRC)
1640 Rhode Island Avenue NW, Washington, DC   20036-3278
(202) 628-4160 • fax: (202) 347-5323
website: www.hrc.org

The Human Rights Campaign (HRC) is the largest civil rights organization dedicated to advancing the rights of lesbian, gay, bisexual, and transgender (LGBT) Americans. For more than thirty years, the organization has helped facilitate grassroots movements, worked to elect politicians whose views coincide with their own, and informed the citizenry at large about LGBT issues. Among other focuses, HRC has worked to legalize marriage for same-sex couples across the nation, seeing legalization as the only means by which equality can truly be achieved. Also, HRC has sought to assist LGBT couples in securing adoptions and protecting same-sex parents' rights. Information about these initiatives, as well as many others directed at ensuring equal rights for LGBT people, can be found on HRC's website.

National Gay and Lesbian Task Force
1325 Massachusetts Avenue NW, Suite 600
Washington, DC   20005
(202) 393-5177 • fax: (202) 393-2241
website: www.thetaskforce.org

The National Gay and Lesbian Task Force is a national organization seeking to increase the presence of lesbian, gay, bisexual, and transgender (LGBT) activism at the grassroots level in rural settings, small towns, and cities with the intent of enacting larger political change and equality for all LGBT people in the nation's capital. Issues focused on by the organization include elections and politics, hate crimes, marriage, and parenting and family. Reports on these topics and many others can be read on the task force's website, and interactive maps showing the varied laws relating to LGBT issues can be viewed there as well.

National Organization for Marriage (NOM)
2029 K Street NW, Suite 300, Washington, DC   20006
(888) 894-3604
e-mail: contact@nationformarriage.org
website: www.nationformarriage.org

Founded as an organization to oppose the growing support for same-sex marriage, the National Organization for Marriage (NOM) has sought to be the centralized voice against gay marriage, particularly in the Northeast and on the West Coast where the practice has become legalized. NOM publications, such as "Is Gay Marriage Good for the Economy?" and "Why Libertarians Should Oppose Same-Sex Marriage," present the case against same-sex marriage; these articles as well as others on the topic can be read on the organization's website.

Servicemembers Legal Defense Network (SLDN)
PO Box 65301, Washington, DC   20035-5301
(202) 328-3244 • fax: (202) 797-1635
e-mail: sldn@sldn.org
website: www.sldn.org

Servicemembers Legal Defense Network (SLDN) began working in 1993 to ensure that lesbian, gay, bisexual, and transgender (LGBT) individuals serving in America's military are treated equally to their heterosexual counterparts and do not experience discrimination based on their sexual orientation or gender identity. While the organization counted as a victory the repeal of the Don't Ask, Don't Tell (DADT) law that restricted homosexuals from openly serving in the armed forces, SLDN believes there is still work to be done to achieve total equality for LGBT service personnel. Visitors to the SLDN site can download the guide "Freedom to Serve: The Definitive

Guide to LGBT Military Service" to find out more information about the continuing bias against LGBT people in the
military, tips for serving, and suggestions about what to do if
one was discharged under the repealed DADT legislation.

Bibliography of Books

M.V. Lee Badgett — *When Gay People Get Married: What Happens When Societies Legalize Same-Sex Marriage.* New York: New York University Press, 2009.

Jacques Balthazart — *The Biology of Homosexuality.* New York: Oxford University Press, 2011.

Aaron Belkin and Geoffrey Bateman, eds. — *Don't Ask, Don't Tell: Debating the Gay Ban in the Military.* Boulder, CO: Lynne Rienner, 2003.

David M. Brodzinsky and Adam Pertman, eds. — *Adoption by Lesbians and Gay Men: A New Dimension in Family Diversity.* New York: Oxford University Press, 2012.

Thomas C. Caramagno — *Irreconcilable Differences?: Intellectual Stalemate in the Gay Rights Debate.* Westport, CT: Praeger, 2002.

John Corvino, ed. — *Same Sex: Debating the Ethics, Science, and Culture of Homosexuality.* Lanham, MD: Rowman & Littlefield, 1997.

John P. De Cecco and David Allen Parker, eds. — *Sex, Cells, and Same-Sex Desire: The Biology of Sexual Preference.* New York: Haworth, 1995.

Vicki L. Eaklor — *Queer America: A GLBT History of the 20th Century.* Westport, CT: Greenwood Press, 2008.

Nathaniel Frank — *Unfriendly Fire: How the Gay Ban Undermines the Military and Weakens America.* New York: Thomas Dunne, 2009.

Evan Gerstmann — *Same-Sex Marriage and the Constitution.* New York: Cambridge University Press, 2008.

Dean Hamer and Peter Copeland — *The Science of Desire: The Search for the Gay Gene and the Biology of Behavior.* New York: Simon & Schuster, 1994.

Stephen Hicks and Janet McDermott, eds. — *Lesbian and Gay Fostering and Adoption: Extraordinary Yet Ordinary.* Philadelphia, PA: J. Kingsley, 1999.

Innocent Himbaza, Adrien Schenker, and Jean-Baptiste Edart — *The Bible on the Question of Homosexuality.* Washington, DC: Catholic University of America Press, 2012.

Erwin W. Lutzer — *The Truth About Same-Sex Marriage: 6 Things You Must Know About What's Really at Stake.* Chicago, IL: Moody Publishers, 2010.

Jeffrey McGowan — *Major Conflict: One Gay Man's Life in the Don't-Ask-Don't-Tell Military.* New York: Broadway Books, 2005.

Jim McKnight — *Straight Science?: Homosexuality, Evolution and Adaptation.* New York: Routledge, 1997.

Frank Mark
Mondimore

A Natural History of Homosexuality.
Baltimore, MD: Johns Hopkins
University Press, 1996.

David G. Myers
and Letha
Dawson Scanzoni

*What God Has Joined Together?: A
Christian Case for Gay Marriage.* New
York: HarperCollins, 2005.

Martha C.
Nussbaum

*From Disgust to Humanity: Sexual
Orientation and Constitutional Law.*
New York: Oxford University Press,
2010.

Nancy D. Polikoff

*Beyond Straight and Gay Marriage:
Valuing All Families Under the Law.*
Boston, MA: Beacon, 2008.

Jonathan Rauch

*Gay Marriage: Why It Is Good for
Gays, Good for Straights, and Good
for America.* New York: Times
Books/Henry Holt and Co., 2004.

Jennifer
Robertson, ed.

*Same-Sex Cultures and Sexualities: An
Anthropological Reader.* Malden, MA:
Blackwell Publishing, 2005.

Josh Seefried, ed.

*Our Time: Breaking the Silence of
"Don't Ask, Don't Tell."* New York:
Penguin, 2011.

Jeffrey S. Siker,
ed.

*Homosexuality and Religion: An
Encyclopedia.* Westport, CT:
Greenwood Press, 2007.

Glenn T. Stanton
and Bill Maier

*Marriage on Trial: The Case Against
Same-Sex Marriage and Parenting.*
Downers Grove, IL: InterVarsity
Press, 2004.

Christopher Wolfe, ed. *Homosexuality and American Public Life.* Dallas, TX: Spence, 1999.

Index

CPSIA information can be obtained
at www.ICGtesting.com
Printed in the USA
FFOW031126280213